Steck-Vaughn
GED
ESSAY

PROGRAM CONSULTANTS

Liz Anderson, Director of Adult Education/Skills Training
Northwest Shoals Community College
Muscle Shoals, Alabama

Mary Ann Corley, Ph.D., Director
Lindy Boggs National Center for Community Literacy
Loyola University New Orleans
New Orleans, Louisiana

Nancy Dunlap, Adult Education Coordinator
Northside Independent School District
San Antonio, Texas

Roger M. Hansard, Director of Adult Education
CCARE Learning Center
Tazewell, Tennessee

Nancy Lawrence, M.A.
Education and Curriculum Consultant
Butler, Pennsylvania

Pat L. Taylor, STARS Consultant for GEDTS
Adult Education/GED Programs
Mesa, Arizona

STECK-VAUGHN
ELEMENTARY · SECONDARY · ADULT · LIBRARY

A Harcourt Company

www.steck-vaughn.com

Acknowledgments

Executive Editor: Ellen Northcutt

Supervising Editor: Julie Higgins

Associate Editor: Sarah Combs

Associate Director of Design: Cynthia Ellis

Designers: Rusty Kaim
Katie Nott

Media Researcher: Sarah Fraser

Editorial Development: Learning Unlimited, Oak Park, Illinois

Production Development: LaurelTech

Photography: Cover: (stack of paper) ©Index Stock; (pencil eraser) ©Laszlo Stern; (pencils and essay) Digital Studios; p.i ©Index Stock; p.14 ©Park Street; p.26 ©Stephanie Heubinger; p.40 ©Michael Newman/PhotoEdit; pp.58, 78 ©Bob Daemmrich Photo, Inc.; p.90 ©Amy C. Etra/PhotoEdit; p.100 ©Mary Pat Waldron; p.110 ©Chuck Savage/The Stock Market.

ISBN 0-7398-2832-0

Contents

What Are the GED Tests?

You have taken a big step in your life by deciding to take the GED Tests. By the time that you have opened this book, you have made a second important decision: to put in the time and effort to prepare for the tests. You may feel nervous about what is ahead, which is only natural. Relax and read the following pages to find out more about the GED Tests in general and the Language Arts, Writing, Part II, The Essay in particular.

The GED Tests are the five tests of General Educational Development. The GED Testing Service of the American Council on Education makes them available to adults who did not graduate from high school. When you pass the GED Tests, you will receive a certificate that is regarded as equivalent to a high school diploma. Employers in private industry and government, as well as admissions officers in colleges and universities, accept the GED certificate as they would a high school diploma.

The GED Tests cover the same subjects that people study in high school. The five subject areas include: Language Arts, Writing and Language Arts, Reading (which, together, are equivalent to high school English), Social Studies, Science, and Mathematics. You will not be required to know all the information that is usually taught in high school. However, across the five tests you will be tested on your ability to read and process information, solve problems, and communicate effectively. Some of the states in the U.S. also require a test on the U.S. Constitution or on state government. Check with your local adult education center to see if your state requires such a test.

Each year more than 800,000 people take the GED Tests. Of those completing the test battery, 70 percent earn their GED certificates. The *Steck-Vaughn GED Series* will help you pass the GED Tests by providing instruction and practice in the skill areas needed to pass, practice with test items like those found on the GED Test, test-taking tips, timed-test practice, and evaluation charts to help track your progress.

There are five separate GED Tests. The chart on page 4 gives you information on the content, number of items, and time limit for each test. Because states have different requirements for how many tests you take in a day or testing period, you need to check with your local adult education center for the requirements in your state, province, or territory.

The Tests of General Educational Development

Test	Content Areas	Items	Time Limit
Language Arts, Writing, Part I	Organization 15% Sentence Structure 30% Usage 30% Mechanics 25%	50 questions	75 minutes
Language Arts, Writing, Part II	Essay		45 minutes
Social Studies	U.S. History 25% World History 15% Civics and Government 25% Geography 15% Economics 20%	50 questions	70 minutes
Science	Life Science 45% Earth and Space Science 20% Physical Science 35%	50 questions	80 minutes
Language Arts, Reading	Nonfiction Texts 25% Literary Texts 75% • Prose Fiction • Poetry • Drama	40 questions	65 minutes
Mathematics	Number Operations and Number Sense 25% Measurement and Geometry 25% Data Analysis, Statistics, and Probability 25% Algebra 25%	Part I: 25 questions with optional use of a calculator Part II: 25 questions without a calculator	90 minutes

In addition to these content areas, you will be asked to answer items based on work- and consumer-related texts across all five tests. These do not require any specialized knowledge, but will ask you to draw upon your own observations and life experiences.

The Language Arts, Reading, Social Studies, and Science Tests will ask you to answer questions by interpreting reading passages, diagrams, charts and graphs, maps, cartoons, and practical and historical documents.

The Language Arts, Writing Test will ask you to detect and correct common errors in edited American English as well as decide on the most effective organization of text. The Essay portion of the Writing Test will ask you to write an essay offering your opinion or an explanation on a single topic of general knowledge.

The Mathematics Test will ask you to solve a variety of word problems, many with graphics, using basic computation, analytical, and reasoning skills.

GED Scores

After you complete each GED Test, you will receive a score for that test. Once you have completed all five GED Tests, you will receive a total score. The total score is an average of all the other scores. The highest score possible on a single test is 800. The scores needed to pass the GED vary depending on where you live. Contact your local adult education center for the minimum passing scores for your state, province, or territory.

Where Can You Go to Take the GED Tests?

The GED Tests are offered year-round throughout the United States and its possessions, on U.S. military bases worldwide, and in Canada. To find out when and where tests are held near you, contact the GED Hot Line at 1-800-62-MY-GED (1-800-626-9433) or one of these institutions in your area:

- An adult education center
- A continuing education center
- A local community college
- A public library
- A private business school or technical school
- The public board of education

In addition, the GED Hot Line and the institutions can give you information regarding necessary identification, testing fees, writing implements, and on the scientific calculator to be used on the GED Mathematics Test. Also, check on the testing schedule at each institution; some testing centers are open several days a week, and others are open only on weekends.

Other GED Resources

- www.acenet.edu This is the official site for the GED Testing Service. Just follow the GED links throughout the site for information on the test.

- www.steckvaughn.com Follow the Adult Learners link to learn more about available GED preparation materials and www.gedpractice.com. This site also provides other resources for adult learners.

- www.nifl.gov/nifl/ The National Institute for Literacy's site provides information on instruction, federal policies, and national initiatives that affect adult education.

- www.doleta.gov U.S. Department of Labor's Employment and Training Administration site offers information on adult training programs.

Why Should You Take the GED Tests?

A GED certificate is widely recognized as the equivalent of a high school diploma and can help you in the following ways:

Employment

People with GED certificates have proven their determination to succeed by following through with their education. They generally have less difficulty changing jobs or moving up in their present companies. In many cases, employers will not hire someone who does not have a high school diploma or the equivalent.

Education

Many technical schools, vocational schools, or other training programs may require a high school diploma or the equivalent in order to enroll in their programs. However, to enter a college or university, you must have a high school diploma or the equivalent.

Personal Development

The most important thing is how you feel about yourself. You now have the unique opportunity to accomplish an important goal. With some effort, you can attain a GED certificate that will help you in the future and make you feel proud of yourself now.

How to Prepare for the GED Tests

Classes for GED preparation are available to anyone who wants to prepare to take the GED Tests. Most GED preparation programs offer individualized instruction and tutors who can help you identify areas in which you may need help. Many adult education centers offer free day or night classes. The classes are usually informal and allow you to work at your own pace and with other adults who also are studying for the GED Tests.

If you prefer to study by yourself, the *Steck-Vaughn GED Series* has been developed to guide your study through skill instruction and practice exercises. *Steck-Vaughn GED Exercise* books and www.gedpractice.com are also available to provide you with additional practice for each test. In addition to working on specific skills, you will be able to take practice GED Tests (like those in this book) in order to check your progress. For information about classes available near you, contact one of the resources in the list on page 5.

What You Need to Know to Pass
Language Arts, Writing, Part II, The Essay

In the Language Arts, Writing Test, Part II, you will be asked to write an essay. An essay is a composition that gives the writer's views on a particular topic. This book will teach you methods to gather and organize ideas, write your essay, evaluate it, and revise it. You will focus on developing a five-paragraph essay, which is an effective way to organize a GED essay. A five-paragraph essay includes an introductory paragraph, three body paragraphs, and a conclusion paragraph.

What Is the Topic Like?

The GED Test will provide you with a brief topic, or prompt. You will be asked to present an opinion or an explanation related to a situation. You will be able to draw on your personal observations, knowledge, and experience to write the essay. One sample GED topic is on page 9 of this introduction. You will also be working with topics similar to the ones on the GED Test as you work through this book.

What Is the Test Format?

You will have 45 minutes to write your essay. Within those 45 minutes, you should plan, write, and proofread your essay. The test booklet will contain scratch paper for planning and two lined pages for the final draft. On pages 8 and 9, you can see the two pages of directions for the test with a sample topic.

How Is the Essay Scored?

A sample of the GED Essay Scoring Guide is on page 10. The process that is used to score the essay is called holistic scoring. Two trained readers score the essay by evaluating its overall effectiveness by judging how well you:

- focus, develop, and support your main points
- organize your essay
- demonstrate effective word choice
- use correct sentence structure, grammar, spelling, and punctuation

Two readers, who each assign a score between 1 and 4, will score your essay. This will result in a total of 2 to 8. This total will be divided by 2, since two readers scored the essay. Therefore, your essay could receive any of the following average scores: 1, 1.5, 2, 2.5, 3, 3.5, or 4. An example of a paper that received a score of 3 is on pages 11–12. An explanation of the score follows the essay.

If anyone receives an average score less than 2, that person must repeat both parts of the Language Arts, Writing Test. If your essay receives a score of 2 or higher, a formula is used to find a combined score for Parts I and II of the Writing Test.

Sample GED Essay Test

Language Arts,
Writing, Part II

Essay Directions and Topic

Look at the box on the next page. In the box are your assigned topic and the letter of that topic.

You must write on the assigned topic ONLY.

You will have 45 minutes to write on your assigned essay topic. You may return to the multiple-choice section after you complete your essay if you have time remaining in this test period. Do not return the Language Arts, Writing booklet until you finish both Parts I and II of the Language Arts, Writing Test.

Two evaluators will score your essay according to its overall effectiveness. Their evaluation will be based on the following features:

- Well-focused main points
- Clear organization
- Specific development of your ideas
- Control of sentence structure, punctuation, grammar, word choice, and spelling

REMEMBER, YOU MUST COMPLETE BOTH THE MULTIPLE-CHOICE QUESTIONS (PART I) AND THE ESSAY (PART II) TO RECEIVE A SCORE ON THE LANGUAGE ARTS, WRITING TEST. To avoid having to repeat both parts of the test, be sure to do the following:

- Do not leave the pages blank.
- Write legibly in ink so that the evaluators will be able to read your writing.
- Write on the assigned topic. If you write on a topic other than the one assigned, you will not receive a score for the Language Arts, Writing Test.
- Write your essay on the lined pages of the separate answer sheet on pages 156–157 of this book. Only the writing on these pages will be scored.

IMPORTANT:
The essay that you write is the property of the GED Testing Service (GEDTS) and is considered confidential and secure. GEDTS policy prohibits your discussing or publicizing the topic or content of your essay. This policy also prohibits returning the essay to you, your family, or any other individual or program.

TOPIC F

If you could make one positive change to your daily life, what would that change be?

In your essay, identify the change you would make. Explain the reasons for your choice.

Part II is a test to determine how well you can use written language to explain your ideas.

In preparing your essay, you should take the following steps:

- Read the **DIRECTIONS** and the **TOPIC** carefully.
- Plan your essay before you write. Use the scratch paper provided to make any notes. These notes will be collected but not scored.
- Before you turn in your essay, reread what you have written and make any changes that will improve your essay.

Your essay should be long enough to develop the topic adequately.

Adapted with permission of the American Council on Education.

GED Essay Scoring Guide

	1 Inadequate	2 Marginal	3 Adequate	4 Effective
	Reader has difficulty identifying or following the writer's ideas.	Reader occasionally has difficulty understanding or following the writer's ideas.	Reader understands writer's ideas.	Reader understands and easily follows the writer's expression of ideas.
Response to the Prompt	Attempts to address prompt but with little or no success in establishing a focus.	Addresses the prompt, though the focus may shift.	Uses the writing prompt to establish a main idea.	Presents a clearly focused main idea that addresses the prompt.
Organization	Fails to organize ideas.	Shows some evidence of organizational plan.	Uses an identifiable organizational plan.	Establishes a clear and logical organization.
Development and Details	Demonstrates little or no development; usually lacks details or examples or presents irrelevant information.	Has some development but lacks specific details; may be limited to a listing, repetitions, or generalizations.	Has focused but occasionally uneven development; incorporates some specific detail.	Achieves coherent development with specific and relevant details and examples.
Conventions of EAE	Exhibits minimal or no control of sentence structure and the conventions of EAE.	Demonstrates inconsistent control of sentence structure and the conventions of EAE.	Generally controls sentence structure and the conventions of EAE.	Consistently controls sentence structure and the conventions of Edited American English (EAE).
Word Choice	Exhibits weak and/or inappropriate words.	Exhibits a narrow range of word choice, often including inappropriate selections.	Exhibits appropriate word choice.	Exhibits varied and precise word choice.

Reprinted with permission of the American Council on Education.

Sample Essay

Topic F

If I could make one positive change in my life, I would be a better communicator. I believe that communication affects our world greatly and that all people should make an extra effort to develop our communication skills. The two major communication skills I wish to improve are listening and speaking.

Listening is one of the most important listening skills. If I could be a better listener, I think I would get more accomplished. By not only hearing but listening to people, I would understand their ideas better. If I would be able to listen to others better, I would have less misunderstanding.

Speaking is another communication skill I would like to improve. If my speaking skills were more enhanced, I believe that I could make others understand my meaning clearer and faster. Speaking would also help me to deal with any misunderstandings that might come up in my life.

Speaking and listening are two important communication skills; I would like to improve in my daily life. I feel that these skills would help me to get more accomplished and eliminate many misunderstandings.

In conclusion, I feel that by improving my communication skills I could change my life for the better. By improving my communication skills, I think that I would not just affect my present but my future.

Commentary on the Sample Essay

SCORE = 3

The essay is <u>understandable</u> and is plainly <u>organized around a main idea based on the prompt</u>—the desire to improve communication as a change in the writer's life. The central idea is given two strands of development—listening and speaking. Although each of these strands is discussed in a direct, understandable paragraph, the author uses vague generalizations and restatements of the author's ideas rather than progressive development with specific details; for example, "Speaking and listening are two important communication skills" and "Listening is one of the most important listening skills." <u>Word choice is appropriate</u> but somewhat monotonous. <u>Sentence structure is under control</u>, although there are usage errors such as "I would have less misunderstandings." and "I could make others understand my meaning clearer and faster." The conventions of <u>EAE [Edited American English]</u> are generally controlled.

The POWER Writing Program

This book gives you the POWER to succeed on the GED essay by providing a step-by-step approach to writing a good five-paragraph essay. In fact, this program is called the POWER program. Each step—from how to begin your essay to how to end it—is listed for you. **P** stands for **Plan**, **O** for **Organize**, **W** for **Write**, **E** for **Evaluate**, and **R** for **Revise**. The chart that follows summarizes the POWER Writing Program.

POWER Writing Steps

Unit		Steps	Time
Planning Your Essay (Pages 14–25)	P	☐ Understanding the Writing Assignment ☐ Gathering Your Ideas ☐ Determining Your Main Idea	5 minutes
Organizing Your Essay (Pages 26–39)	O	☐ Grouping and Labeling ☐ Expanding Your Groups ☐ Ordering Your Groups	5 minutes
Writing Your Essay (Pages 40–57)	W	☐ The Three Parts of an Essay ☐ Paragraphs and Topic Sentences ☐ Writing Your Introductory Paragraph ☐ Writing Body Paragraphs ☐ Developing Body Paragraphs ☐ Writing Your Concluding Paragraph	25 minutes
Evaluating Your Essay (Pages 58–77)	E	☐ Holistic Scoring ☐ Evaluating an Essay	5 minutes
Revising Your Essay (Pages 78–89)	R	☐ Revising Ideas and Organization ☐ Editing for the Conventions of English	5 minutes

In this book you will get plenty of practice with each of the POWER steps. Review the POWER steps until they become automatic for you and use them as you write the essays in this book. Following the time limits will allow sufficient time for you to write a good essay and check it within the 45-minute time limit on the test.

Also, work with the Writer's Handbook on pages 128–141 to improve your mastery of the conventions of English that are important for both Part I and Part II.

Planning

On Part II of the GED Language Arts, Writing Test, you will have 45 minutes to write an essay on an assigned topic. Because you are expected to write only one draft, you should spend about five minutes planning your essay. Thinking about the topic and then gathering ideas, examples, and supporting details are critical in creating a successful GED essay.

That is why the first step in the POWER writing process is planning. In this unit, you will learn how to understand the essay topic and to gather ideas about the topic. You will learn to gather your ideas by making lists and idea maps. Then you will look at all of your ideas to see what they have in common so that you can develop a main idea for your essay.

Planning helps you achieve your goals.

Kerri Richards
Function Manager

Organizing
Your Essay

Writing
Your Essay

Evaluating
Your Essay

Revising
Your Essay

Planning Your Essay

- Understanding the Writing Assignment
- Gathering Your Ideas: Making a List
- Gathering Your Ideas: Making an Idea Map
- Determining Your Main Idea

The lessons in this unit include:

Lesson 1: **Understanding the Writing Assignment**
Understanding the writing assignment will help you decide what kind of information is needed in your essay.

Lesson 2: **Gathering Your Ideas: Making a List**
You will need to gather ideas for your essay. One method for gathering ideas is to make a list.

Lesson 3: **Gathering Your Ideas: Making an Idea Map**
Another method for organizing your ideas is to make an idea map. An idea map shows the relationship between ideas.

Lesson 4: **Determining Your Main Idea**
Once you have gathered ideas, you will choose the main idea of your essay.

Read each GED writing assignment. Then underline key words and write the kind of information you should give. Use the chart on page 16 to help you.

TOPIC 1

What is a true friend?

Write an essay that describes what a true friend is. Use your personal observations, experience, and knowledge to support your view.

Kind of information: _____

TOPIC 2

Some people believe it is harmful for both parents of a preschool child to work outside the home, others do not feel this way.

State your point of view in an essay. Give specific examples to support your view. Use your personal observations, experience, and knowledge.

Kind of information: _____

TOPIC 3

How does the climate in your region affect you and the other people who live there?

Write an essay explaining both the advantages and disadvantages of living in your climate. Use your personal observations, experience, and knowledge to support your view.

Kind of information: _____

TOPIC 4

Despite laws that require people to wear seat belts, many people still do not wear them.

Write an essay that explains why people do not buckle up. Use your personal observations, experience, and knowledge to support your view.

Kind of information: _____

TOPIC 5

How important is having a GED or a high-school diploma when you apply for a job?

In an essay, tell your point of view. Give specific examples to support your view. Use your personal observations, experience, and knowledge.

Kind of information: _____

Answers start on page 142.

GED SKILL Gathering Your Ideas: Making a List

gathering ideas
when a writer lists related ideas about a topic to support a main idea

list
when a writer jots down ideas in the order he or she thinks of them

Once you understand the writing assignment, you are ready to begin **gathering ideas.** For your essay to get a good score, you need a variety of specific ideas and examples. Use your own observations, experience, and knowledge to gather ideas that you can write about easily.

To gather ideas, spend about five minutes thinking about the topic and writing down all the ideas that come to mind. Then stop and review what you have written. This review may help you think of more ideas.

One way to record your ideas is to make a **list.** When you make a list, you write your ideas in the order you think of them.

Look at the list of ideas one student made for the essay topic below. Add three ideas of your own.

TOPIC: Has modern technology made our lives better or worse?

Topic: Effects of modern technology
medical advances extend life
more efficiency in workplace
environment is polluted
transportation is better
people have lost touch with nature
computers invade our privacy

_____

_____

_____

TIP

Don't worry about having enough ideas for an essay. Relax and write down every idea that comes to mind. Your first ideas may not be your best ideas, so don't stop at two or three.

Any idea you added is correct if it relates to the topic. You might have added *better communication, more forms of entertainment, housework is easier, more free time, more stress due to a faster pace of life, people are less active,* or *fewer personal relationships.*

Read each essay topic. Then list as many ideas as you can. Try to list at least five or six ideas for each topic.

TOPIC 1: How watching television affects people

TOPIC 2: How being a sports fan affects your life

TOPIC 3: The importance of having a GED or high-school diploma

TOPIC 4: The influence of popular music on young people

Answers start on page 142.

GED SKILL Gathering Your Ideas: Making an Idea Map

idea map
a way of recording ideas that shows their relationship to the topic and to each other

TIP

When you have finished your idea map, look at each idea you have connected to the topic and think about it. That will help you gather new ideas.

Another way to record your ideas for an essay is to make an **idea map.** When you make an idea map, you write down ideas in a way that shows their relationship to the topic and to each other.

To make an idea map, write your topic in the middle of a piece of paper and draw an oval around it. As you think of each new idea, write it down, draw an oval around it, and connect it to the idea to which it relates. You will find that some of your ideas are closely related to the topic itself, while others are more related to other ideas you have written.

Look at one student's idea map for the topic below. Then draw an oval and add an idea of your own.

TOPIC: *How can you take an affordable trip?*

Any idea you added is correct if it relates to the topic. You might have added *take day trips and sleep at home, make bag or picnic lunches,* or *travel with friends and split the costs.* Check to be sure that you put your idea in a logical place. For instance, if you wrote *make bag or picnic lunches,* you should have put it in an oval that was attached to the *Food* oval.

A. Read each essay topic. Then fill in the idea map with ideas. Add ovals to the map if you need to.

TOPIC 1: The benefits of regular exercise

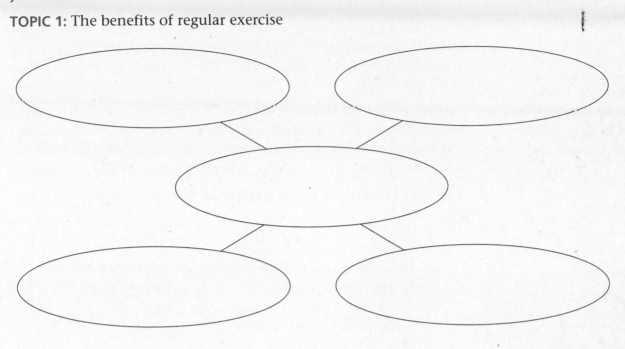

TOPIC 2: The similarities and differences between men's and women's personalities

B. Read each essay topic. Make an idea map for each topic. Draw your own maps or make copies of the blank idea map on page 128.

TOPIC 3: Causes of stress in modern life

TOPIC 4: Ways to save money on your food bill

Answers start on page 142.

GED SKILL Determining Your Main Idea

main idea
the most important point you are trying to make

After you gather ideas on a topic, you need to determine the **main idea** of your essay. The main idea is the most important point you are trying to make about the topic. To determine your main idea, look at all your ideas and try to figure out what they have in common.

For example, if the topic is about the positive and negative effects of technology, see if your ideas are mostly positive effects, negative effects, or both. If you wrote mostly positive effects, your main idea might be *Overall, technology has had many positive effects on society.*

Look at the list of ideas gathered for this topic.

TOPIC: Are there more advantages or disadvantages to owning a car?

> have to pay for insurance
> pollutes the air more than public transportation
> buying and upkeep cost more than taking the bus
> can go where you want, when you want
> not always easy to find parking
> have privacy in a car

TIP

Your main idea should be one sentence that is broad enough to cover all your supporting ideas.

Put a check mark by the sentence that best states the main idea of this list.

_____ (a) Owning a car has many advantages.

_____ (b) Car ownership has many disadvantages.

Most of the ideas relate to the problems that car owners have. Therefore, a good main idea for this list would be *option (b).*

Read the topic and ideas below. Write a main idea statement.

TOPIC: Is it better to own or rent your home?

> renters have to depend on the landlord for repairs
> buying a home is a good investment
> if you own, you're responsible for repairs and maintenance
> renters can be forced to move when lease is up
> rents can increase suddenly
> have to pay property taxes if you own

Main idea statement: _____

_____

Most of the ideas listed are advantages of owning a home. Therefore, your main idea statement should be something like *Owning your home is better than renting.*

A. Read the topic and ideas below. Write a main idea statement.

TOPIC: Causes of homelessness

> living paycheck to paycheck, costly crisis happens
> drug use
> abused kids go live on the street
> not enough low-income housing available

Main idea statement: _____

B. Look at the lists of ideas that you wrote on page 19. Write a main idea statement for each list.

TOPIC 1: How watching television affects people

Main idea statement: _____

TOPIC 2: How being a sports fan affects your life

Main idea statement: _____

TOPIC 3: The importance of having a GED or high-school diploma

Main idea statement: _____

TOPIC 4: The influence of popular music on young people

Main idea statement: _____

C. Look at the idea maps that you made on page 21. Write a main idea statement for each idea map.

TOPIC 1: The benefits of regular exercise

Main idea statement: _____

TOPIC 2: The similarities and differences between men's and women's personalities

Main idea statement: _____

TOPIC 3: Causes of stress in modern life

Main idea statement: _____

TOPIC 4: Ways to save money on your food bill

Main idea statement: _____

Answers start on page 142.

Unit 1 Cumulative Review **Planning**

Review your understanding of planning skills by answering the questions about the sample GED essay topic below.

> **TOPIC**
>
> Is life better in a city or in a small town?
>
> Explain your point of view in an essay. Use your personal observations, experience, and knowledge to support your view.

1. Underline the key words in the instructions.

2. What kind of information do these key words tell you to include in your essay?

   _____

   _____

3. Think about the topic. What are two methods that you could use to gather your ideas about this topic?

   _____

   _____

   _____

4. Once you have gathered ideas on the topic, see what the ideas have in common. What do you do once you recognize what your ideas have in common?

   _____

   _____

   _____

   _____

Answers start on page 142.

Because you will have only 45 minutes to write your GED essay, try to spend about five minutes planning it. On this Mini-Test, see how much planning you have done at the end of five minutes. If you need to finish, do so, but keep in mind that you need to work on planning your essay in five minutes.

Remember, at this point you are only gathering ideas for this essay. You will continue to work on the essay as you work through this book.

Read the GED essay assignment below. Follow the steps you learned in this unit to gather ideas for an essay. <u>Do not write the essay; do only the planning stage.</u>

TOPIC

Is life better in a city or in a small town?

Explain your point of view in an essay. Use your personal observations, experience, and knowledge to support your view.

Think About POWER Step 1 ·····································

When you have finished planning your essay on the topic above, answer these questions.

1. Were you able to think of many ideas?

2. Was it easy or difficult to think of ideas?

3. Did you list ideas or make an idea map? Did this method seem to work for you?

4. Was it easy or difficult to choose a main idea statement?

 Save your planning work for this essay topic. If you like, begin a Writing Portfolio—a folder where you will keep your writing—and put this essay plan there. You will be developing an essay over several units, and you need to save your work and come back to it.

If you had trouble gathering ideas and would like to learn other methods that may work better for you, be sure to read Lesson 18, "More Ways to Gather Ideas."

· ·

In Unit 2, you will learn how to organize your ideas.

Answers start on page 142.

Organizing

You have learned how to gather ideas for your GED essay. Now you need to develop your ideas in a way that will make sense to the reader. Before you start writing your essay, you should spend about five minutes organizing your ideas.

That is why the second step in the POWER writing process is organizing. In this unit, you will learn how to divide your ideas into groups and how to label the groups. Because an effective GED essay depends on having many good ideas and examples, you will also practice expanding your groups of ideas. In addition, you will learn how to put your idea groups in logical order. When you begin writing your essay, these idea groups will become the basis for your paragraphs.

Making a list helps you organize any task.

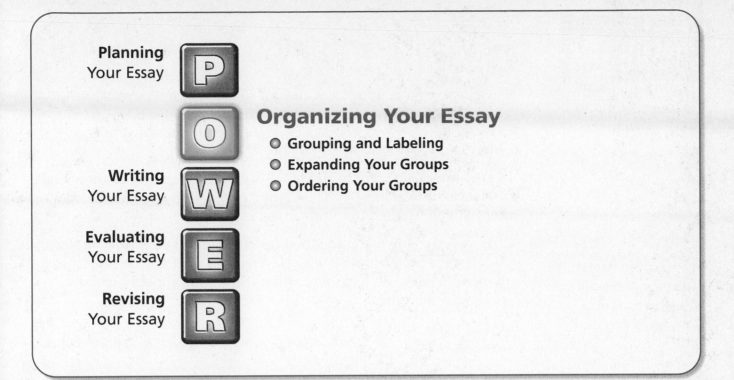

Planning Your Essay

Writing Your Essay

Evaluating Your Essay

Revising Your Essay

Organizing Your Essay

- Grouping and Labeling
- Expanding Your Groups
- Ordering Your Groups

The lessons in this unit include:

Lesson 5: **Grouping and Labeling**
To organize your essay, you will need to group and label your ideas. Each group of ideas will become a paragraph that supports the main idea of your essay.

Lesson 6: **Expanding Your Groups**
You may not think of all your best ideas at once. After you have listed and grouped ideas about a topic, you can use one or more strategies to add more ideas.

Lesson 7: **Ordering Your Groups**
There are several ways to organize your ideas in a logical manner. One method is arranging ideas in the order of their importance. The other method is comparing and contrasting different ideas.

GED SKILL **Grouping and Labeling**

Once you have some ideas about a topic, your next step is **grouping the ideas** and **labeling the groups.** Each group of ideas will become a paragraph that supports the main idea of your essay.

To group ideas, see what the ideas on your list have in common. Put these ideas in a group and label, or name, the group to show how it relates to the main idea. Then group other related ideas and label them. If an idea does not fit in any group, cross it out.

Here is the way one student grouped her ideas about how watching TV affects people, a topic you worked with in Unit 1. First, she listed all the ideas that came to mind without thinking about how they related to each other.

Get rid of unrelated ideas before you start writing. This can keep you on the topic.

<u>Main idea:</u>   Watching TV has both good and bad effects.

<u>The Effects of Watching TV</u>
violence seems to be everywhere
keeps people from reading
keeps people from spending time
   with family
keeps people from doing active things
TVs cost a lot
informs
provides an escape from everyday life
entertainment
ads make people want things

Next, she looked for ways to group her ideas. To do this, she looked for ideas that were related. She knew she had listed both good and bad effects, so she circled all the ideas that were good effects and labeled them. Then she did the same for the bad effects. The labels helped her remember what the ideas in each group had in common.

After sorting out her ideas, she realized that one idea—*TVs cost a lot*—was not an effect at all, so she crossed that idea off her list.

GED SKILL Understanding the Writing Assignment

writing assignment directions to write about a given topic

The **topic** is the subject of your essay. All the ideas in your essay should relate to this topic.

You do not need any specialized knowledge to write a GED essay.

The second part of the GED Language Arts, Writing Test is a **writing assignment** for an essay. This test requires you to state your view on a **topic** and to support that view with examples. For instance, here is a typical GED writing assignment.

> Has modern technology, such as the computer, made people's lives better or worse?
>
> Write an essay to explain your view on that topic. Use your personal observations, experience, and knowledge to support your view.

The **instructions** tell what kind of information to give in your essay.

The key words *explain your view* tell what you should do in your essay. This chart contains key words commonly used in essay instructions that are clues to the kind of information you should give.

If the instructions say	You should
explain why state the reasons	write about causes or reasons
explain the effects discuss the advantages and disadvantages	write about effects
describe	discuss the qualities of something
state your position present your view give your opinion	tell what you think about an issue and why

discuss the similarities and
    differences
compare and contrast
	explain how things are alike
	    and different

Read this GED writing assignment and underline the instructions. Then answer the question that follows.

Why is fast food so popular?

In an essay, state the reasons for fast food's popularity. Use your personal observations, experience, and knowledge to support your view.

What kind of information is needed? _____

You were correct if you wrote *causes* or *reasons*.

The student's groups of ideas looked like this:

The Effects of Watching TV

violence seems to be everywhere

keeps people from reading

keeps people from spending time with family

keeps people from doing active things

Bad effects

TVs cost a lot

informs

provides an escape from everyday life

entertainment — Good effects

ads make people want things

Try to make three groups of ideas. Having three groups will help ensure you have enough support for your main idea.

It is usually not difficult to divide your list of ideas into two groups. However, because you want to write a five-paragraph essay, it is best to have three groups of related ideas. These three groups will contain the ideas for the three middle, supporting paragraphs of your essay. If you divide your larger group into two groups, each of your three groups can become a supporting paragraph of your essay.

To make her three groups, the student noticed that she could make two groups from the larger group—*the bad effects of TV*. One group could include things that were unrealistic about TV. The other could include things that watching TV kept people from doing.

Bad Effects

False Sense of Life

want too many things (ads)

violence seems to be everywhere

Keeps People from Better Things

reading

family

doing active things

If the writer had used an idea map, many of her ideas would already be grouped and connected. She would need only to label the different groups, like this:

Ask yourself if the ideas in each group have something in common and if the labels tell how the ideas are related.

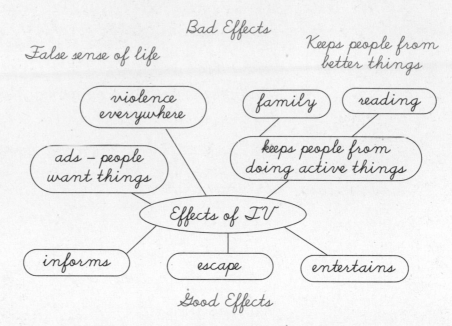

Read the three groups of ideas for the topic "What are the pros and cons of having a hobby?" Put a check mark next to the idea that does not fit with any of the groups. In which group does the other idea belong?

_____ (a) bowling is my hobby

_____ (b) may become too involved, lose interest in other things

The Pros and Cons of Having a Hobby

Pros		Cons
Practical Reasons	**Emotional or Social Reasons**	
can learn things	have fun	may neglect things that need to be done
can develop new skills	relieve stress	
	may meet people with similar interests	may spend too much money

You were correct if you chose *option* (*a*) because it does not fit in any of the groups. *Option* (*b*) belongs in the group *Cons* because it is another possible negative effect of having a hobby.

A. Read the writing assignment and make a list of ideas. If you prefer to make an idea map, you may draw your own or make copies of the blank idea map on page 128.

> Why are pets so important to their owners? Support your ideas with examples.

_____   _____

_____   _____

_____   _____

_____   _____

_____   _____

_____   _____

_____   _____

B. If you listed your ideas, sort and rewrite the ideas into three groups below. Label each group. If you made an idea map, label the groups.

_____   _____   _____

_____   _____   _____

_____   _____   _____

_____   _____   _____

_____   _____   _____

_____   _____   _____

_____   _____   _____

_____   _____   _____

Answers start on page 142.

GED SKILL Expanding Your Groups

All your best ideas may not come to mind at once. Therefore, after you have listed and grouped ideas about a topic, see if you can add more. Try using one of these methods to think of more ideas:

- Reread the topic, your main idea, and your groups of ideas.
- Ask *who, what, when, where, why,* and *how* about the topic.
- Think about how the topic affects you or people you know.
- Try to think of things you have read or heard about the topic.

The student who wrote about the effects of watching TV used these methods. When she reread her second group of bad effects— *keeps people from doing other things*—she thought about how people may watch TV to avoid dealing with problems. She added that idea to her list.

To expand her group of good effects, she asked herself questions:

- Who watches TV? *everyone—adults, teens, kids*
- What do they watch? *adults and teens watch comedies, news, action shows; kids watch educational shows, cartoons*
- Why do they watch? *to learn, to be entertained, to escape*

The student also considered how TV affected her and people she knew. She had learned about safe dieting on TV, and her niece had learned the alphabet from *Sesame Street.*

Look at the student's expanded groups. Her new ideas are in color. Put a check mark by the idea you could add to one of the groups.

____ (a) You use a program guide to check times and channels for TV programs.

____ (b) You read that TV can give children unrealistic ideas about the effects of violence.

TIP

To think how a topic affects you, try to recall experiences you or people you know have had that are related to the topic.

Bad Effects	*Good Effects*
False Sense of Life—want too many things; violence seems to be everywhere	*Information—news programs give current events and health information; educational shows teach*
Keeps People from Better Things—reading; family; doing active things; dealing with problems	*Entertainment and Escape— comedies, cartoons, action shows*

You were correct if you chose *option (b)*. That could be added to *False Sense of Life* under *Bad Effects*.

A. Expand the groups of ideas by answering the questions below. Then add your ideas to the lists.

Main idea statement: Swimming is a good sport.

Benefits	**Little Equipment**	**Ease and Convenience**
exercise	swimsuit	can do year-round
fun	towel	park district pools

_____ _____ _____

_____ _____ _____

_____ _____ _____

_____ _____ _____

- *Who* can go swimming?
- *What* do you need to go swimming?
- *When* can you go swimming?
- *Where* can you go swimming?
- *Why* do people go swimming?

B. Use different methods for expanding groups to add ideas to these groups.

TOPIC: What effect would passing the GED Tests have on a person?

Personal	**Job-related**	**Educational**
feel good about yourself	get a more satisfying job	stronger reading and
learn how not to quit	earn more money	math skills
		chance to go on to college

_____ _____ _____

_____ _____ _____

_____ _____ _____

C. On page 31, you grouped ideas for the topic "Why are pets so important to their owners?" Use one of the methods listed on page 32 to expand your groups of ideas.

Answers start on page 143.

GED SKILL Ordering Your Groups

You need to take one more step before you write your essay. You must choose a logical order in which to present your groups. Because each of your three groups of ideas will become a paragraph in your essay, the order is important. You want the paragraphs ordered in a way that makes your essay strong and convincing.

There are several ways to order ideas. For a GED essay, two useful methods are order of importance and compare and contrast.

Order of Importance

order of importance
a method of essay writing that starts with the least important ideas and ends with the most important

You can rank your groups of ideas from least important to most important and write about them in **order of importance.** Because this kind of organization builds from the weakest ideas to the strongest ideas, the last thing a reader sees and the thing that stays in a reader's mind is the most important point.

The paragraphs below are from an essay about seat belt laws. The ideas are in order of importance. Notice how the words in color help you, the reader, understand the order of ideas.

Seat belt laws are a source of money for cities. People ticketed for not wearing seat belts must pay fines, and this money can be used for roadway maintenance.

Even more important, seat belt laws improve traffic safety. Just by buckling up, people are reminded to drive more safely.

But the most important reason that seat belt laws are wise is that they save lives. Countless numbers of people are alive today because they were wearing their seat belts when they had accidents. Countless more have been saved from serious injury.

The writer placed his reasons for supporting seat belt laws in order from least important to most important. The most important reason, saving lives, is the last one to be read. It leaves you, the reader, with the strongest impression.

Try reading the paragraphs in the opposite order of the way they are written. How does it change the effectiveness of the essay?

TIP

These words signal that ideas are organized in order of importance: *more important, most important, better, best.*

_____

_____

If you read the most important reason first, the other reasons seem less significant. But when you read the least important reason first, it seems valid, and each additional reason adds to the argument.

Compare and Contrast

compare and contrast
a method of organizing the ideas in an essay to show how two things are alike and different

contrast
to discuss different sides of a topic

When you compare things, you show how they are alike. When you contrast things, you show how they are different. A GED writing assignment may ask you to **compare and contrast** two things, such as the problems of the past and those we encounter today. Or it may ask you to **contrast** different sides of a topic, such as the advantages and disadvantages (or pros and cons) of a night-shift job.

The student organized her essay about the effects of watching TV by contrasting the positive and negative effects. Pay attention to the phrases in color. They show how the ideas are ordered.

There is no doubt that watching television can have positive effects. Adults can keep informed about current events by watching the evening news. They may even gain some practical knowledge about their health and other personal concerns. Children can learn from educational shows like *Sesame Street.* In addition, everyone can be entertained and even escape a little with cartoons, comedies, and action shows.

On the other hand, watching television has some definite negative effects. Instead of just using it as a temporary escape, some people may watch television rather than deal with their problems. TV also keeps people from spending time with their family or from reading. In fact, it turns some people into couch potatoes, keeping them from any physical activity.

In addition, television gives people a false sense of what life is like. They see commercials on TV and feel they must have what's being advertised. They see violence on shows and think modern life is more violent than it really is, or they may even think it is all right to act violently.

By contrasting the negative and positive effects of watching television, the student got her main idea across effectively. She used her first paragraph to discuss the good effects. She used her second paragraph to discuss some of the bad effects, and she signaled this contrast with the words *on the other hand.* She used her third paragraph to discuss more negative effects.

Try reading the paragraphs in the opposite order of the way they are written. How does it change the effectiveness of the essay?

_____

_____

A writer's strongest arguments should come near the end of the essay. Because there are more negative effects than positive effects—enough for two paragraphs—placing them last focuses attention on them. When the paragraph on positive effects is placed at the end, the essay is less effective. It weakens the writer's negative view of TV. Is that how you felt as you read the paragraphs in the opposite order?

These words signal a comparison: *both, also, similarly, like.* These words signal a contrast: *on the other hand, in contrast, however, but, whereas, while.*

Which Organization Should You Use?

The method of organization you choose to present your ideas should give the greatest support to your main idea. This chart can help you decide.

If you are writing about	Try using
reasons or causes good or bad effects the qualities of one thing how you feel about an issue	order of importance
good and bad effects advantages and disadvantages	contrast
the qualities of two things	compare and contrast

Before you decide how to order groups for an essay, write your main idea at the top of your paper. That will keep you focused on the main idea and help you decide the best way to support it.

The paragraphs about seat belts on page 34 listed reasons for wearing seat belts, so the writer used order of importance. The essay about watching television on page 35 discussed good and bad effects of television, so the writer used contrast. The example below describes the qualities of two friends, so the writer used compare and contrast. Pay attention to the signal words in color.

My friend Jamie and I have a lot in common. Both of us are very adventurous. We love to try new things, such as different foods, and we enjoy outdoor sports, like in-line skating. We also share a passion for country music.

Both of us work in a restaurant, but we don't do exactly the same job. I'm a short-order cook in a coffee shop, and Jamie is a waiter in a Mexican restaurant.

Though we are good friends, we are different in some ways. Jamie grew up in a large family, but I am an only child. I have always lived in New York while Jamie was born in a small town in Ohio, but he has lived all over the country.

Read the ideas for the following essay topic. What method of organization would you choose for the essay?

TOPIC: Why do people still smoke despite the known dangers?

> relieves tension
> teenagers think it's cool
> the hazards don't seem real
> still acceptable in some places
> people don't want to be told what to do
> advertising makes smoking look glamorous

Best organization: _____

You were correct if you chose *order of importance*. The list of ideas gives reasons that people smoke.

A. For each essay topic, determine the method of organization and the order of ideas you think would best support the main idea. Number the groups in that order. For Topics 2 and 3, write a main idea statement.

TOPIC 1: What are the qualities of swimming that make it worthwhile?

Main idea statement: Swimming is a worthwhile sport.

Organization: _____

Benefits ____	**Little Equipment** ____	**Ease and Convenience** ____
healthy exercise	swimsuit	can do year-round
little stress on body	towel	park district pools
fun	maybe swimming goggles	beach in summer
mental relaxation		easy to learn

TOPIC 2: What effect would passing the GED Tests have on a person?

Main idea statement: _____

Organization: _____

Personal Reasons ____	**Job-Related Reasons** ____	**Educational Reasons** ____
feel good about yourself	get a more satisfying job	stronger reading and
learn how not to quit	earn more money	math skills
more confidence	better chance for promotion	chance to go on to college

TOPIC 3: What are the positive and negative effects of society's emphasis on being thin?

Main idea statement: _____

Organization: _____

Bad Effects on Society ____	**Good Effects on Health** ____	**Bad Effects on Individuals** ____
children learn to make fun of overweight people	many people eat well and exercise	feel bad about yourself if not thin
people judge by appearance	fewer health problems	some become obsessed with thinness
overweight people are discriminated against	fewer medical costs related to obesity	some try unsafe diets
		could lead to anorexia

B. Review the groups of ideas you wrote for the essay topic "Why are pets so important to their owners?" on pages 31 and 33. Decide on the best method of organization, and number the groups in the order you would write about them.

Answers start on page 143.

Unit 2 Cumulative Review **Organizing**

Review your understanding of organizing skills by answering the questions about the sample GED essay topic below.

TOPIC

Is life better in a city or in a small town?

Explain your point of view in an essay. Use your personal observations, experience, and knowledge to support your view.

1. You have already made a list of ideas or an idea map for this topic. What should be your first step in organizing those ideas?

   _____

   _____

2. What methods can you use to think of more ideas?

   _____

   _____

   _____

   _____

   _____

3. What is the best kind of organization for an essay like this one? Why?

   _____

   _____

4. In what order would you put your three groups? Why?

   _____

   _____

   _____

Answers start on page 143.

Because you will have only 45 minutes to write your GED essay, try to spend about five minutes organizing it. On this Mini-Test, see how much organizing you have done at the end of five minutes. If you need to finish, do so, but keep in mind that you need to work on organizing your essay in five minutes.

Remember, at this point you are only organizing your ideas for this essay. You will continue to work on the essay as you work through this book.

Refer to the essay that you planned on page 25 for the following topic. Follow the steps you learned in this unit to organize the ideas that you gathered on that topic. Do not write the essay; just organize the ideas.

TOPIC

Is life better in a city or in a small town?

Explain your point of view in an essay. Use your personal observations, experience, and knowledge to support your view.

Think About POWER Step 2 ••••••••••••••••••••••••••••••••••

When you have finished organizing your essay on the topic above, answer these questions.

1. Were you able to group and label your ideas easily?

2. Was it easy or difficult to expand your groups?

3. Did you choose the best organization for your ideas?

You may save the ideas that you organized for this essay in your Writing Portfolio. You will use this material again in the Mini-Test at the end of the next unit.

If you had trouble organizing ideas and would like to learn other methods that may work better for you, be sure to read Lesson 19, "More Ways to Organize Ideas."

• •

In Unit 3, you will learn how to write the first draft of an essay.

Answers start on page 143.

UNIT 3

Writing

After you plan and organize your thoughts and ideas, you will be ready to write. That is why the third step in the POWER process is writing your essay. You should spend about 25 minutes writing the first draft of your essay.

In this unit, you will learn to write the three parts of the essay—the introduction, body, and conclusion. The introductory paragraph states the topic of the essay. The body paragraphs develop the topic, and the concluding paragraph ties the whole essay together. You will also learn how to develop good topic sentences that express the main ideas of your paragraphs. A strong introduction, body, and conclusion are the basics of an effective essay.

Writing is a way to communicate your ideas.

Planning Your Essay

Organizing Your Essay

Writing Your Essay

- The Three Parts of an Essay
- Paragraphs and Topic Sentences
- Writing Your Introductory Paragraph
- Writing Body Paragraphs
- Developing Body Paragraphs
- Writing Your Concluding Paragraph

Evaluating Your Essay

Revising Your Essay

The lessons in this unit include:

Lesson 8: **The Three Parts of an Essay**
An essay has three basic parts: an introduction, a body, and a conclusion.

Lesson 9: **Paragraphs and Topic Sentences**
Each paragraph in an essay is organized around one main idea with supporting sentences.

Lesson 10: **Writing Your Introductory Paragraph**
An introductory paragraph tells the reader the main idea of the essay in a thesis statement, and it previews the rest of the essay.

Lesson 11: **Writing Body Paragraphs**
The body paragraphs develop the topic with supporting ideas.

Lesson 12: **Developing Body Paragraphs**
An effective essay has well-developed ideas. This means that the writer provides examples, reasons, and details.

Lesson 13: **Writing Your Concluding Paragraph**
The concluding paragraph gives the same information that the introductory paragraph gives, but instead of previewing the information, it reviews it.

GED SKILL The Three Parts of an Essay

An essay has three basic parts: an introduction, a body, and a conclusion, in that order. Each part has a specific purpose. In a five-paragraph essay, each part also consists of a specific number of paragraphs.

To write a five-paragraph essay in preparation for the GED Test, one student read the following topic and then completed the first two POWER steps. Read the topic and look at his lists of ideas.

Is regular exercise important in maintaining good health?

Write an essay explaining your point of view. Use your personal observations, experience, and knowledge.

Main idea: *Regular exercise is important.*

Better Health	Look Better	Feel Better
stronger heart	lose weight	feel good about
breathe better	firm muscles	how you look
more endurance	healthier skin	more self-esteem
burns calories	and hair	reduces tension
		feel more relaxed

Then the student wrote the following essay. Read it and notice how the three parts of an essay are contained in the five paragraphs.

Introduction
- one paragraph
- includes the essay topic
- tells the main idea

Many people exercise regularly, yet many others do not. If those who don't exercise knew how important it is, they would all start exercise programs. Regular exercise makes and keeps you fit. In fact, it helps you look and feel fit in addition to being fit.

Body
- three paragraphs
- develops the topic
- supports the main idea

First of all, regular exercise is good for your health. When you run, bicycle, or do some other aerobic activity regularly, your heart becomes stronger, and your breathing improves. These physical changes increase your endurance. You actually have more energy. Also, muscles that are working burn more fat calories.

Exercise can help improve not only your health but also your looks. Because your body burns more calories, you lose weight and look slimmer and trimmer. Your muscles become firm. You seem more youthful and energetic. In addition, better circulation gives your skin and hair a healthy glow.

All these physical benefits lead to perhaps the most important result of regular exercise—it makes you feel better. Exercise reduces tension in your muscles and makes you more relaxed. You feel rested and ready to go during the day, and you sleep better at night. Because you look better, you also feel better about your body and about yourself. Your self-esteem increases.

With all these benefits of regular exercise, it's hard to understand why someone would <u>not</u> work out. If you exercise regularly, your body and your mind will appreciate it.

GED SKILL **Paragraphs and Topic Sentences**

Before you write your essay, you need to know how to develop a good paragraph. To do so, focus on the groups of ideas you wrote in POWER Step 2. Each group will become a paragraph in your essay.

topic sentence
the sentence that tells the main idea of the paragraph

supporting details
additional ideas that give more information about the main idea

Each paragraph will have a **topic sentence** that tells the main idea of the paragraph. The other ideas become the **supporting details** of the paragraph. You can write the topic sentence at the beginning, middle, or end of a paragraph. A paragraph may be written in these three ways:

Topic Sentence – Supporting Details

Supporting Details – **Topic Sentence** – Supporting Details

Supporting Details – **Topic Sentence**

Read the following paragraphs. Where are the topic sentences?

1. The cost of living has risen steadily over the past several decades. While a loaf of bread cost 30 cents 40 years ago, today it can cost six or seven times that. Just 30 years ago, you could purchase a new car for about $4,000. Today the average cost of a new car is closer to $14,000. The price of housing is another example of rising costs. In the 1960s, an apartment rented for as little as $125 a month. With today's rents, that same apartment would cost at least $600 per month.

2. Many city pools are open for free or for just a few dollars admission during the summer. Picnics are a great way to enjoy the outdoors, especially on cool summer evenings. Some local parks have theater productions or live music for free—you only need to bring your lawn chair. Recreational centers provide a variety of activities for all ages, from movies to bowling. Amusement parks and long vacations may be the summer tradition, but even a family on a budget can have a great summer.

The first sentence of paragraph 1 is the topic sentence. It tells the main idea of the paragraph. The rest of the sentences support the paragraph's main idea with details that contrast the prices of bread, cars, and housing. In paragraph 2, the topic sentence is the last sentence. It states the main idea of the paragraph.

Read each paragraph. Then answer the questions.

1.   A good worker is someone who understands how important it is not to be absent too often and who gets the job done. People seldom get fired because the quality of their work is poor. Instead, more people lose their jobs for such things as not showing up for work or not doing their job. Managers need to know that they can count on their workers to be on the job. Employers have little tolerance for workers who talk so much with their co-workers that they can't finish a job.

    a. What is the paragraph about? _____

_____

    b. Underline the topic sentence.

    c. List some supporting details. _____

_____

_____

_____

_____

2.   Over the years people have moved into much of the wilderness area where bald eagles live. Eagles build their nests in the tops of tall trees near water. More and more of that land has become farmland or city streets, and the pollution of lakes and rivers has poisoned the fish that eagles eat. As a result, the bald eagles have had problems reproducing. They lay eggs that don't hatch. In addition, until 1950 hunters and trappers were allowed to kill many bald eagles. It is ironic that Americans are directly responsible for making the bald eagle, their national bird, an endangered species.

    a. What is the paragraph about? _____

_____

    b. Underline the topic sentence.

    c. List some supporting details. _____

_____

_____

_____

_____

Answers start on page 143.

Each paragraph below has supporting details but no topic sentence. Circle the letter of the best topic sentence for each paragraph.

1.   Some companies put coupons or rebate offers in newspapers or send them through the mail. Other companies place coupons or rebate offers right on the packaging. The companies hope consumers will buy their products because of these offers. The value of a coupon is subtracted from the cost of the item when it is purchased. To get a rebate, a consumer must send a receipt and a product label to the company and wait for a rebate check in the mail. Shoppers can save money by taking advantage of these manufacturer incentives.

   a. Consumers can make ends meet by buying generic brands and taking advantage of coupon offers.

   b. Many manufacturers try to increase sales by offering money-saving coupons or rebates.

   c. Manufacturers should lower the cost of their products rather than use coupons to get shoppers to buy their products.

2.   In a crime-stoppers program, someone may be paid for supplying information that leads to the arrest and conviction of a person who commits a felony. The identity of the person who reports information is kept secret so that no harm will come to him or her. Funds to support this crime-stoppers program come from tax dollars as well as private contributions. This effort has assisted many communities in solving criminal cases.

   a. An organization will reward people who report information about crimes that have been committed.

   b. Crime is increasing in this country at an alarming rate, and something has to be done about it.

   c. There is a better way to fight crime than relying on taxpayers' dollars.

3.   Even before you have an interview, your résumé may give a prospective employer a first impression of you. An employer may screen out an applicant with a résumé that makes a bad impression. A résumé should be neatly typed and easy to read. It should also be complete enough to tell important information about you. If it is organized well, it can be thorough without being too long; one page is preferred. You can use underlining, capital letters, and asterisks to point out important information you would like an employer to know.

   a. A résumé is a tool that can help you get a job interview.

   b. When you have an interview for a job, you should tell about all your past work experience.

   c. Even if you have a great résumé, you won't get the job if you arrive late for an interview.

Answers start on page 144.

Write a topic sentence for each paragraph.

1.   Two hundred years ago, few people could read or write. At that time, people could get jobs and make a living without having to read or to write their names. However, over the years, jobs have become more complex and complicated. Machinery and technology have replaced workers that once performed manual labor. The ability to think has become much more important. Jobs that require workers to read, write, compute, and think have become the norm.

_____

_____

_____

2.   Smoking cigarettes is bad for your health. In fact, tobacco use in any form has been proven harmful. Thousands of people die each year from lung cancer, and thousands more die from heart disease that is linked to smoking. In addition, smoking is an expensive habit. Heavy smokers may spend as much as $7 per day on cigarettes. That adds up to about $210 a month! Think of all the things a person could buy with that money.

_____

_____

_____

3.   There are consumer groups you may go to for financial help. They will review your finances and advise you on how to reduce your debt. They will help you make a budget to pay your creditors. They will even tell you if your financial situation is so complicated that you need to see an attorney. People to whom you owe money will often work with you as well. They may be willing to reduce your monthly payments so that you can afford to pay them. Most important, you can learn to live within your means.

_____

_____

_____

4.   Pharmacists do not generally mark a prescription drug with an expiration date, although the container usually shows the date of the prescription. Generally, you should not take a drug if it is more than one year old. A good rule to remember about the length of time to keep prescription drugs is, "When in doubt, throw it out."

_____

_____

_____

Answers start on page 144.

GED SKILL **Writing Your Introductory Paragraph**

thesis statement
a sentence that tells the topic of an essay

preview sentences
sentences in the introduction that tell your reader what to expect in the essay

TIP

Sometimes your main idea becomes clearer after you've planned your essay. Your thesis statement can pinpoint exactly what you want to say.

A good **introductory paragraph** does several things:
* It tells what your topic and main idea are.
* It gives a preview of your essay.
* It may provide background information.

The topic of an essay is stated in a sentence called the **thesis statement.** This sentence is the main idea of the whole essay. You can write the thesis statement by rewriting your main idea from POWER Step 1. Expand the main idea by adding words that help explain or strengthen the statement. This example shows how a student expanded her main idea into a thesis statement.

Main idea: I like TV comedies.
Thesis statement: Of all the many different kinds of TV shows, comedies are my favorite.

A good introductory paragraph has one or more **preview sentences.** Preview sentences tell your reader what to expect in the essay. To write preview sentences, use your labeled groups, from POWER Step 2, and tell about them in a brief, general, and interesting way.

Finally, you can add one or two **background sentences** that give general information about the topic. Background sentences are not necessary, but they can help introduce your topic.

Here is the introductory paragraph from the essay on pages 42–43. In the planning stage, the main idea was "Regular exercise is important."

Underline the thesis statement. Circle the preview sentence.

Many people exercise regularly, yet many others do not. If those who don't exercise knew how important it is, they would all start exercise programs. Regular exercise makes and keeps you fit. In fact, it helps you look and feel fit in addition to being fit.

The thesis statement is *Regular exercise makes and keeps you fit.* The preview sentence is *In fact, it helps you look and feel fit in addition to being fit.* It tells in general what the three middle paragraphs of the essay are about. The first two sentences of the introduction are background information.

Write introductory paragraphs for the topic assignments below. Follow these steps.

a. Read each topic assignment. Use POWER Steps 1 and 2 to create groups of ideas, label them, and write a main idea for each topic. Topic 1 has been done for you. Use it as a model.

b. Write an introductory paragraph for each essay. Use a separate sheet of paper for each topic.

TOPIC 1

Is it fair for professional athletes to receive such high salaries?

Explain your viewpoint in an essay. Use your personal observations, experience, and knowledge.

Main idea: Athletes earn their money.

Physical Work	**Professionals**	**Serve the Community**
requires intense training	train for a long time	act as positive role models
can be hurt or hospitalized	work hard to become pro	do commercials against drugs
chance of long-term injury	have to stay on a strict diet	work for charities
lots of effort during game	have no privacy	

TOPIC 2

How does rock music influence young people?

Write an essay that explains positive influences, negative influences, or both. Use your personal observations, experience, and knowledge.

TOPIC 3

What is the role of being a parent?

Write an essay that discusses the responsibilities, the pleasures, or both. Explain your view with details and examples. Use your personal observations, experience, and knowledge.

Answers start on page 144.

GED SKILL Writing Body Paragraphs

Now you're ready to write the **body paragraphs** of your essay. The three body paragraphs develop your topic. They back up the thesis statement in your introductory paragraph with supporting ideas.

To write three body paragraphs, use your expanded groups of ideas from POWER Step 2. Follow the order you chose for the groups. Use the label you gave to the first group to help you write a topic sentence for that paragraph. Then use the ideas from the group to write supporting sentences for the paragraph. To be sure your supporting sentences stay on the topic, keep your list handy as you write.

Follow those same steps to write your next two body paragraphs.

Here are the body paragraphs from the essay about exercise on pages 42–43. Compare the paragraphs with the three groups of ideas. Notice how each underlined topic sentence tells the main idea of the paragraph. Notice also that the writer has added details that aren't in the groups. While he was writing the body paragraphs, new ideas occurred to him.

You can place a topic sentence at the beginning, middle, or end of a paragraph, but it's a good idea to put it first so that your reader knows what the paragraph is about.

<u>Better Health</u>

stronger heart
breathe better
more endurance
burns calories

<u>First of all, regular exercise is good for your health.</u> When you run, bicycle, or do some other aerobic activity regularly, your heart becomes stronger, and your breathing improves. These physical changes increase your endurance. You actually have more energy. Also, muscles that are working burn more fat calories.

<u>Look Better</u>

lose weight
firm muscles
healthier skin
and hair

<u>Exercise can help improve not only your health but also your looks.</u> Because your body burns more calories, you lose weight and look slimmer and trimmer. Your muscles become firm. You seem more youthful and energetic. In addition, better circulation gives your skin and hair a healthy glow.

Feel Better

feel good about
 how you look
more self-esteem
reduces tension
feel more relaxed

All these physical benefits lead to perhaps the most important result of regular exercise—it makes you feel better. Exercise reduces tension in your muscles and makes you more relaxed. You feel rested and ready to go during the day, and you sleep better at night. Because you look better, you also feel better about your body and about yourself. Your self-esteem increases.

TIP

You can use new ideas that occur to you during any of the POWER steps. Just be sure they support the thesis statement of the essay as well as the topic sentence of the paragraph.

Look at the first group of ideas on page 49 for the essay on athletes' salaries. On a separate sheet of paper, write a topic sentence. Then write supporting sentences.

Compare your work with this sample body paragraph. The topic sentence is underlined: _A professional athlete's job requires demanding physical work._ Athletes must train intensely to keep in shape. They put forth a great deal of effort during every game. In addition, athletes may be hurt during the course of a game, and their injuries may require hospitalization. The possibility of long-term injury is a constant threat.

GED SKILL FOCUS

Use your work from the GED Skill Focus on page 49. Follow these steps for each topic assignment. Use the same paper that you used to write the introductory paragraphs.

a. Review the lists of ideas and the introductory paragraph you wrote.

b. Follow the order you chose for the lists.

c. Use the labels to write topic sentences.

d. Use the ideas in the group to write supporting sentences.

e. Add details as they come to you.

1. Write three body paragraphs justifying the high salaries of professional athletes.

2. Write three body paragraphs about whether rock music is a bad influence on young people, a positive influence, or both.

3. Write three body paragraphs about the responsibilities of being a parent, the pleasures, or both.

Answers start on page 144.

Lesson 12 GED SKILL Developing Body Paragraphs

TIP

Remember you can correct mistakes in spelling, punctuation, or grammar after you get your ideas down.

To write an effective essay, you need to develop your ideas. To **develop** means to explain with details and examples.

When you develop the ideas in a body paragraph, you provide support for the paragraph's topic sentence. In turn, the three topic sentences of the body paragraphs support the thesis statement of your entire essay. In this way, you write a strong essay.

See how the writer of the essay on exercise gave support to some of his original ideas by adding details to explain them.

Supporting Ideas	Details in Body Paragraph
• burns calories	muscles that are working burn more fat calories
• lose weight	you lose weight and look slimmer and trimmer

An example names a person or explains a situation that helps illustrate what you mean. Read these examples that the writer added to the essay on exercise to illustrate his supporting ideas.

Supporting Ideas	Examples in Body Paragraph
• regular exercise	running, bicycling, or some other aerobic activity regularly
• feel more relaxed	you feel rested and ready to go during the day, and you sleep better at night

In the essay on athletes' salaries, one of the supporting ideas in the third paragraph is: "Athletes act as positive role models."

To develop this idea, think of an athlete who acted as a positive role model. What did he or she do?

_____

_____

A possible answer is *By admitting that he was HIV positive, basketball player Magic Johnson helped reduce the stigma of the disease.*

A. Rewrite each statement below, adding more details to the supporting idea. If you want help thinking of details, use the questions that follow each statement.

1. Sleep is important. (Why is it important? How does it make you feel? What does lack of sleep do to you? What happens when you sleep?)

_____

_____

_____

2. Honesty is the best policy. (Why should people be honest? What are some situations in which honesty plays an important part? What can happen if one is dishonest? Are there times when it is better not to be honest? What would happen if most people were routinely dishonest?)

_____

_____

_____

B. Add one or more examples to each statement below. If you want help thinking of examples, use the questions that follow.

3. Our lives are filled with noise. (What kinds of noises are involved? Who or what makes the noises?)

For example, _____

_____

_____

4. People are sometimes rude. (Who in particular is sometimes rude? What do they do that is rude?)

For example, _____

_____

_____

C. Add details and examples to develop the paragraphs you wrote about athletes' salaries, rock music, and parenting. Ask yourself questions to help you think of additional details and examples. Add them in the margins or rewrite the paragraphs.

Answers start on page 144.

Lesson 13

GED SKILL Writing Your Concluding Paragraph

The last paragraph of your essay is the **concluding paragraph.** It gives the same information that the introductory paragraph gives, but it is written from a different perspective. Instead of previewing the ideas in your essay, a concluding paragraph reviews them. It restates your thesis statement and sums up your supporting ideas. For example, reread the concluding paragraph from the essay about exercise.

With all these benefits of regular exercise, it's hard to understand why someone would <u>not</u> work out. If you exercise regularly, your body and your mind will appreciate it.

The thesis statement in the introductory paragraph was *Regular exercise makes and keeps you fit.* The last sentence in the concluding paragraph restates this idea as *If you exercise regularly, your body and your mind will appreciate it.*

The supporting details in the essay discussed three benefits of exercise—better health, looking better, and feeling better. These details are summed up in the phrase *With all these benefits of regular exercise.*

Finally, the conclusion also includes this strong statement about the topic that leaves an impression in the reader's mind: *it's hard to understand why someone would <u>not</u> work out.*

Reread the introductory and body paragraphs you wrote for the essay on athletes' salaries on pages 49 and 51. Write a concluding paragraph for the essay on the same paper.

Here is a possible concluding paragraph:
Professional athletes provide us with hours of entertainment as well as valuable service to the community, and they work extremely hard to make that possible. Considering what athletes contribute, their high salaries are more than justified. In fact, they should be paid even more.

Your concluding paragraph may be different, but it should restate your thesis statement and sum up the three main ideas from your three body paragraphs. You might also have included a strong, last-impression statement.

TIP

As you write your essay, you may want to add or change phrases or sentences. Leave wide margins so that you can make changes easily.

Look back at the introductory and body paragraphs you wrote for the essays on rock music and parenting on pages 49 and 51. Then complete the exercises below.

1. Write a concluding paragraph for the essay about the ways that rock music influences young people.

_____

_____

_____

_____

_____

_____

_____

_____

2. Write a concluding paragraph for the essay about the responsibilities, the pleasures, or both of being a parent.

_____

_____

_____

_____

_____

_____

_____

_____

_____

Answers start on page 144.

Unit 3 Cumulative Review **Writing**

Review your understanding of writing a first draft by answering the questions about the sample GED essay topic below.

TOPIC

Is life better in a city or in a small town?

Explain your point of view in an essay. Use your personal observations, experience, and knowledge to support your view.

---

1. What are the three parts you would include in an essay on this topic?

   _____

   _____

2. What kind of information should be in the introductory paragraph?

   _____

   _____

   _____

3. How would you decide on how many body paragraphs you should write?

   _____

   _____

   _____

4. How would you write the topic sentence and supporting details for the body paragraphs?

   _____

   _____

   _____

5. What kind of information should be in the concluding paragraph? How is it different from the introductory paragraph?

   _____

   _____

   _____

Answers start on page 144.

Because you will have only 45 minutes to write your GED essay, try to spend about 25 minutes writing the first draft of your essay. If you need to take more time on this Mini-Test, you may, but keep in mind that you need to work on completing the first draft in 25 minutes.

Refer to the ideas that you organized on page 39 for the following topic. On a separate sheet of paper, follow the steps you learned in this unit to write a first draft for an essay on the topic.

TOPIC

Is life better in a city or in a small town?

Explain your point of view in an essay. Use your personal observations, experience, and knowledge to support your view.

Think About POWER Step 3 ································

When you have finished writing your essay on the topic above, answer these questions.

1. Does your introductory paragraph effectively preview the rest of your essay?

2. Have you organized your paragraphs into main ideas with supporting details?

3. Does your conclusion refer to your thesis statement?

 Save your draft for this essay topic. If you like, put it in your Writing Portfolio. You will use this material again in the Mini-Test at the end of the next unit.

If you would like some additional tips on writing a first draft, be sure to read Unit 7, "Raising Your Score."

In Unit 4, you will learn how to evaluate your essay.

Answers start on page 145.

Evaluating

When you have finished writing a draft of your GED essay, be sure to look for ways to revise and improve it. In the next unit, you will learn more about revising your essay. Once you have submitted your essay, trained essay scorers read it and assign a score. That's why the fourth step in the POWER writing process is evaluating your essay.

In this unit, you will learn about how your essay will be evaluated. You will learn about holistic scoring, the method that the essay scorers use to judge the overall effectiveness of your essay. You will also learn to use the criteria in the GED Essay Scoring Guide to evaluate the effectiveness of essays.

Use any kind of evaluation as an opportunity to improve.

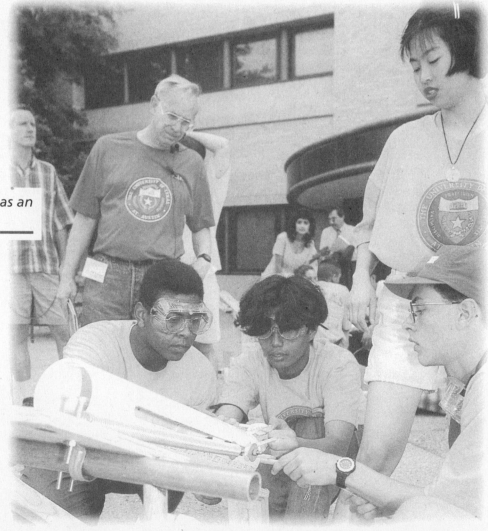

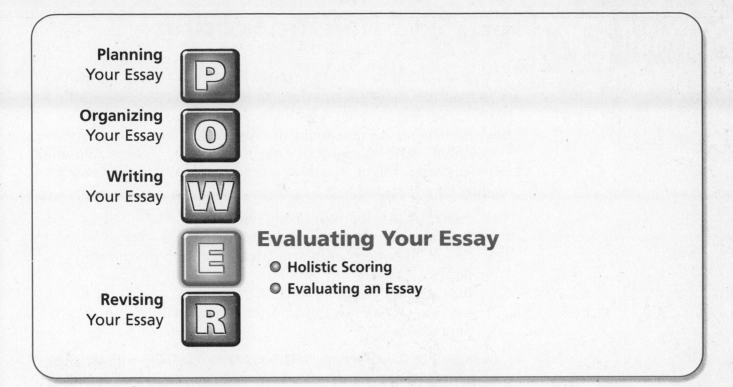

Evaluating Your Essay

- Holistic Scoring
- Evaluating an Essay

The lessons in this unit include:

Lesson 14: **Holistic Scoring**
GED scorers will evaluate your essay by judging its overall effectiveness. This is called scoring holistically. This lesson contains a copy of the scoring guide that will be used to score your essay.

Lesson 15: **Evaluating an Essay**
GED essay scorers will judge your essay by looking at how well you respond to the prompt (the topic), organize and develop your ideas, and give supporting details and examples. They will also look at your sentence structure, usage, and word choice. In this lesson, you will learn more about the GED essay scoring criteria by evaluating other essays.

GED SKILL **Holistic Scoring**

Your essay will be scored **holistically.** This means that it will be judged on its overall effectiveness. To the essay scorers, the most important aspects of your essay are how clearly you present your thesis statement and how well you support it. A few errors in spelling or grammar will not cause your essay to receive a low score, although too many errors might. The essay scorers will evaluate your essay by judging how well you:

- focus and develop your main points
- organize your essay
- provide specific examples and details to support your main points
- use clear and precise word choice
- use correct sentence structure, grammar, spelling, and punctuation

A sample of the complete GED Essay Scoring Guide with detailed explanations of the characteristics that the evaluators look for when they read an essay can be found on page 10.

Essays that are scored 1 or 1.5 are considered failing and that person must repeat both the multiple choice and essay parts of the GED Language Arts, Writing Test. If your essay scores a 2 or above, a formula is used to find a combined score for Parts I and II of the Writing Test.

Read this sample essay and the score it would likely receive.

TOPIC

Is life better in a city or in a small town?

Explain your point of view in an essay. Use your personal observations, experience, and knowledge to support your view.

Life in the big city, and life in a small town vary sharply. There are advantages as well as disadvantages to life in the city, just as there are good and bad things about small towns.

Some of the bad points to city life are high crime, over crowded housing, and heavy traffic. Life can also be very rewarding in the city, as there are more places of employment as well as intertainment.

Life in a small town moves at a slower rate. The people are friendlier, because of a lower crime rate. The housing is spaced more openly, and the highways are not as crowded, because there are less intertainment and employment oppurtunities.

In my oppinion life in the small town far out weighs life in the city because life at a slower pace is more rewarding.

This essay would likely receive a score of 2. It has organization, but the introduction does not address the topic directly by stating whether the writer believes life is better in a small town or a city. There are also some errors in the conventions of English—mainly in spelling.

Look at the scoring guide on page 10 and read about the development and details in an essay that scores 2. Compare that description with the essay above. What is another reason this essay received a 2?

The essay does not develop the details. It merely lists details in the first body paragraph and repeats them in the second body paragraph.

In the next lesson, you will read essays and practice scoring them holistically.

Lesson 15

GED SKILL **Evaluating an Essay**

Five areas are considered when evaluating a GED essay—response to the prompt, organization, development and details, conventions of Edited American English (sentence structure, usage, spelling, capitalization, and punctuation), and word choice. You can use this checklist to help you evaluate your essay.

TIP

Trained GED evaluators read an essay once and then assign a score to it. However, when you evaluate your essay, read it more than once to see how to improve it and get a higher score.

Yes	No	**Response to the Prompt**
☐	☐	(1) Is there a clear main idea?
☐	☐	(2) Does the essay stick to the topic?

Organization

Yes	No	
☐	☐	(3) Does the introductory paragraph include a thesis statement and a preview?
☐	☐	(4) Does each body paragraph have a topic sentence and details related to the topic sentence?
☐	☐	(5) Does the concluding paragraph restate the thesis statement and review the ideas?
☐	☐	(6) Are there smooth transitions between paragraphs and between sentences?

Development and Details

Yes	No	
☐	☐	(7) Do the paragraphs include specific details and examples that support the topic sentences?
☐	☐	(8) Does the essay support the thesis statement?
☐	☐	(9) Is the essay free of irrelevant details?

Conventions of Edited American English

Yes	No	
☐	☐	(10) Are the ideas written in complete sentences?
☐	☐	(11) Is there a variety of sentence structures?
☐	☐	(12) Do all the subjects and verbs agree?
☐	☐	(13) Are verbs in the correct tense?
☐	☐	(14) Are punctuation marks used correctly?
☐	☐	(15) Are words spelled correctly?
☐	☐	(16) Are capital letters used correctly?

Word Choice

Yes	No	
☐	☐	(17) Is the use of words varied and appropriate?
☐	☐	(18) Are words used precisely?

TIP

When you evaluate your GED essay, read it carefully to be sure that your ideas are presented clearly. Ask yourself, "Would another reader understand what I am writing?"

To evaluate your essay, read it at least twice. During the first reading, concentrate on the first three areas of the checklist—response to the prompt, organization, and development and details. These questions help you evaluate your presentation of ideas. During the second reading, concentrate on the last two areas of the checklist— the conventions of Edited American English and word choice.

The six essays on this and the following pages were written for the writing assignment on page 61, living in a city versus living in a small town. Work independently or with a partner to evaluate the essays. Use these steps to evaluate them.

1. Read each essay once to evaluate it as a GED evaluator would. Use the GED scoring guidelines on page 60 to assign a score of 1 to 4.

2. Evaluate each essay again to improve the presentation of ideas. Answer the questions in the first three areas of the checklist that follows each essay.

3. Check over the essay a third time to evaluate the control of the conventions of English and word choice. Answer the questions in the last two areas of the checklist that follows each essay.

Essay 1

If one were to contemplate the advantages and disadvantages of city living versus country or small town living various aspects of both scenerios should be equally eveluated, with fairness to pros and cons alike.

City living for instance has several good points, when you dwell in the city (city-dwellers) as they are called, are people surrounded by convenience, their work place their homes, schools and shopping are within the peramiters or just on the outskirts of the city itself. This lends a tremendous advantage of locality, gives an edge to the city dwellers, as everything is right there within reach, they don't have far to go to get from point 'a' to point 'B' so to speak.

On the other hand, the disadvantages are also plentiful. there are traffic jams almost constantly. Most always smog surrounds the city with an unhealthy shroud of various pollutants, many of wich are harmful to breath on certain days when it is exceptionally thick. The crime rate is higher in big urban cities, many people are in transient and just drifting through, on their way to who knows where?

Drugs are always in the picture, many big time dealers prefer the city as it gives them a wider variety of people to deal their venom to. Children get caught up in the horrible scenerio, drugs and drug related problems plauge big cities. Because of all these neggitive things people are looking to smaller towns and country living to sort of get away from the overcrowding and anonaminity that city living entails. smaller towns by contrast have almost as many ammenities as their bigger more overcrowded counter-parts, people seem to interact better, there is a sense of belonging, small town folk are most always better adjusted. they have fewer problems, you might say they do have some of the problems of the bigger cities but certainly on a much smaller scale.

We as a people have to contend with whatever modes of living nessitates our survival, sometimes we have no choice in where we would prefer to live as in where we actually have to live. Jobs in the 80's often dictate our locale, a lot of times we get a job transfer taking us to various localities. military people for instance must relocate periodically. It is my feeling that one must make the best of a city or town and as a people we most always can etch out a good standard of living whereverrver we live.

Essay 1

○   ○   ○   ○
1   2   3   4

Yes	No	
		Response to the Prompt
☐	☐	(1) Is there a clear main idea?
☐	☐	(2) Does the essay stick to the topic?
		Organization
☐	☐	(3) Does the introductory paragraph include a thesis statement and a preview?
☐	☐	(4) Does each body paragraph have a topic sentence and details related to the topic sentence?
☐	☐	(5) Does the concluding paragraph restate the thesis statement and review the ideas?
☐	☐	(6) Are there smooth transitions between paragraphs and between sentences?
		Development and Details
☐	☐	(7) Do the paragraphs include specific details and examples that support the topic sentences?
☐	☐	(8) Does the essay support the thesis statement?
☐	☐	(9) Is the essay free of irrelevant details?
		Conventions of Edited American English
☐	☐	(10) Are the ideas written in complete sentences?
☐	☐	(11) Is there a variety of sentence structures?
☐	☐	(12) Do all the subjects and verbs agree?
☐	☐	(13) Are verbs in the correct tense?
☐	☐	(14) Are punctuation marks used correctly?
☐	☐	(15) Are words spelled correctly?
☐	☐	(16) Are capital letters used correctly?
		Word Choice
☐	☐	(17) Is the use of words varied and appropriate?
☐	☐	(18) Are words used precisely?

I think that rural life is better than urban. Because you save time and money. You don't have to go to the grocery store as much. You don't have to commute back & forth on a bus. You can do your washing on hand. It is less complicated. The crime rate is very low. Less traffic. Don't worry that much about being mugged or robbed because the town is so small. The people within the community. They seem very nice. The atmosphere smells very clean.

Essay 2

Yes   **No**

Response to the Prompt

☐   ☐   (1)   Is there a clear main idea?

☐   ☐   (2)   Does the essay stick to the topic?

Organization

☐   ☐   (3)   Does the introductory paragraph include a thesis statement and a preview?

☐   ☐   (4)   Does each body paragraph have a topic sentence and details related to the topic sentence?

☐   ☐   (5)   Does the concluding paragraph restate the thesis statement and review the ideas?

☐   ☐   (6)   Are there smooth transitions between paragraphs and between sentences?

Development and Details

☐   ☐   (7)   Do the paragraphs include specific details and examples that support the topic sentences?

☐   ☐   (8)   Does the essay support the thesis statement?

☐   ☐   (9)   Is the essay free of irrelevant details?

Conventions of Edited American English

☐   ☐   (10)   Are the ideas written in complete sentences?

☐   ☐   (11)   Is there a variety of sentence structures?

☐   ☐   (12)   Do all the subjects and verbs agree?

☐   ☐   (13)   Are verbs in the correct tense?

☐   ☐   (14)   Are punctuation marks used correctly?

☐   ☐   (15)   Are words spelled correctly?

☐   ☐   (16)   Are capital letters used correctly?

Word Choice

☐   ☐   (17)   Is the use of words varied and appropriate?

☐   ☐   (18)   Are words used precisely?

City Dwells, for year's and year's this city founders have started to move from the complicated population and noice cities of America to slower and busyless life in small towns. the citizens make a very good decitions for heathy life and tranquility on rural town in to big forest filled with beatiful bird songs and quiet nights. Out from the cars noice and smoked factorys with trash on the streets accidents on the roads, crimes bad situations with frenetized people and dark skys poluted with gases poisining the city trees and litte birds destroy human life slowly but efectivily like some to hardful venom contaminaded lakes and parks with chemicals and drug's. Drug's! the most dengerous numer one problem on the big's city can destroy families and poisoning the young's and the oldest to! but move to small town have little problems for the comfort and comodity on restaurants theaters and quikly movement to one place to other but with this little diference the small town's is the big diference to the big troubles on the populed city.
Welcome to the forest.

Essay 3

○   ○   ○   ○
1   2   3   4

Yes	No	
		Response to the Prompt
☐	☐	(1) Is there a clear main idea?
☐	☐	(2) Does the essay stick to the topic?
		Organization
☐	☐	(3) Does the introductory paragraph include a thesis statement and a preview?
☐	☐	(4) Does each body paragraph have a topic sentence and details related to the topic sentence?
☐	☐	(5) Does the concluding paragraph restate the thesis statement and review the ideas?
☐	☐	(6) Are there smooth transitions between paragraphs and between sentences?
		Development and Details
☐	☐	(7) Do the paragraphs include specific details and examples that support the topic sentences?
☐	☐	(8) Does the essay support the thesis statement?
☐	☐	(9) Is the essay free of irrelevant details?
		Conventions of Edited American English
☐	☐	(10) Are the ideas written in complete sentences?
☐	☐	(11) Is there a variety of sentence structures?
☐	☐	(12) Do all the subjects and verbs agree?
☐	☐	(13) Are verbs in the correct tense?
☐	☐	(14) Are punctuation marks used correctly?
☐	☐	(15) Are words spelled correctly?
☐	☐	(16) Are capital letters used correctly?
		Word Choice
☐	☐	(17) Is the use of words varied and appropriate?
☐	☐	(18) Are words used precisely?

Essay 4

Persons living in the city have certain advantiges over persons living in small towns.

Persons starting their own companies, almost always do better in the big city rather than starting componies in small town. For example, population is greater there is more demand, more demand means a stonger company This also makes it a little easier on the unemployed a stronger company needs more workers.

Also persons living in the city have good times by going out dancing and eating at fancy places, going bowling, seeing movies at the cinema, driving the town and meeting other people and maybe meeting other friends, just plain having a good time.

Persons living in small towns have a simple and good life because thats where they have always lived and made a fair living, but cities allover the United States will always do better than small towns because the more power, and money, and activities for residents the better the recovery in hard times.

Essay 4

○   ○   ○   ○
1   2   3   4

Yes	No	
		Response to the Prompt
☐	☐	(1) Is there a clear main idea?
☐	☐	(2) Does the essay stick to the topic?
		Organization
☐	☐	(3) Does the introductory paragraph include a thesis statement and a preview?
☐	☐	(4) Does each body paragraph have a topic sentence and details related to the topic sentence?
☐	☐	(5) Does the concluding paragraph restate the thesis statement and review the ideas?
☐	☐	(6) Are there smooth transitions between paragraphs and between sentences?
		Development and Details
☐	☐	(7) Do the paragraphs include specific details and examples that support the topic sentences?
☐	☐	(8) Does the essay support the thesis statement?
☐	☐	(9) Is the essay free of irrelevant details?
		Conventions of Edited American English
☐	☐	(10) Are the ideas written in complete sentences?
☐	☐	(11) Is there a variety of sentence structures?
☐	☐	(12) Do all the subjects and verbs agree?
☐	☐	(13) Are verbs in the correct tense?
☐	☐	(14) Are punctuation marks used correctly?
☐	☐	(15) Are words spelled correctly?
☐	☐	(16) Are capital letters used correctly?
		Word Choice
☐	☐	(17) Is the use of words varied and appropriate?
☐	☐	(18) Are words used precisely?

Essay 5

In spite of the obvious advantages of big city life, I'll take the small town everytime. Life in a small town is superior because of the quality of the relationships you can develop and because small town life is less stressful.

The quality of the relationships one can develop in a small town are far better than those that you have in a large, faceless city. People in small towns can really get to know one another. They help each other out and share in each others successes. They have time for one another. People in small towns don't have to fear strangers and can trust others. They can count on there being someone there for them even if they are new to town or have no family close by. People in small towns tend have the time to express their affection for each other. They are more open and giving. It is easier get to know and be known by people in a small rural setting.

In addition the lifestyle in a small town is much less stressful than that of a large city. People seems to be in less of a hurry. There are no crowds to shove and pressure you. Traffic is not a daily nightmare. Crime is not so very plentiful. Drugs don't tempt your children in every corner. These things that create stress in the life of an urban dweller are just not present in the lives of people living in small towns.

Because relationships are easier to develop in a small town and stress is far less noticeable, life in the small town seems superior to living in a city. I'd pick the rural life if I had my choice.

Essay 5

○   ○   ○   ○
1   2   3   4

Yes   **No**   **Response to the Prompt**

☐   ☐   (1)   Is there a clear main idea?

☐   ☐   (2)   Does the essay stick to the topic?

Organization

☐   ☐   (3)   Does the introductory paragraph include a thesis statement and a preview?

☐   ☐   (4)   Does each body paragraph have a topic sentence and details related to the topic sentence?

☐   ☐   (5)   Does the concluding paragraph restate the thesis statement and review the ideas?

☐   ☐   (6)   Are there smooth transitions between paragraphs and between sentences?

Development and Details

☐   ☐   (7)   Do the paragraphs include specific details and examples that support the topic sentences?

☐   ☐   (8)   Does the essay support the thesis statement?

☐   ☐   (9)   Is the essay free of irrelevant details?

Conventions of Edited American English

☐   ☐   (10) Are the ideas written in complete sentences?

☐   ☐   (11) Is there a variety of sentence structures?

☐   ☐   (12) Do all the subjects and verbs agree?

☐   ☐   (13) Are verbs in the correct tense?

☐   ☐   (14) Are punctuation marks used correctly?

☐   ☐   (15) Are words spelled correctly?

☐   ☐   (16) Are capital letters used correctly?

Word Choice

☐   ☐   (17) Is the use of words varied and appropriate?

☐   ☐   (18) Are words used precisely?

I prefer to live in a small town. Rural life is more relaxed and less expensive than life in a large city.

The pace of life in a small town is far more relaxed than ~~life~~ living in a large city. People are not in such a hurry in a small town. They have time for one another and for the little pleasures in life. Because there are fewer people, there are shorter lines at the bank, the grocery, and the post office. People don't get so tense because these everyday activities take less time than in a big city. Drivers don't get stuck in traffic and worry about being late for appointments. This little things add up to fewer hassles and a more relaxed atmosphere.

The cost of living in a big city is a disadvantage, too. ~~Rural~~ Housing in rural towns is cheaper and food cost less. Kids don't go to private schools much so education is not as much. There are fewer reasons to have to dress up and buying clothes is not so important. Keeping up with the Jones is not nearly so important. People can just be theirselves.

Living in a small town is a more relaxed and less expensive way to live. I would rather live in a small town anyday.

Essay 6

○   ○   ○   ○
1   2   3   4

Yes	No	
		Response to the Prompt
☐	☐	(1) Is there a clear main idea?
☐	☐	(2) Does the essay stick to the topic?

Organization

☐	☐	(3) Does the introductory paragraph include a thesis statement and a preview?
☐	☐	(4) Does each body paragraph have a topic sentence and details related to the topic sentence?
☐	☐	(5) Does the concluding paragraph restate the thesis statement and review the ideas?
☐	☐	(6) Are there smooth transitions between paragraphs and between sentences?

Development and Details

☐	☐	(7) Do the paragraphs include specific details and examples that support the topic sentences?
☐	☐	(8) Does the essay support the thesis statement?
☐	☐	(9) Is the essay free of irrelevant details?

Conventions of Edited American English

☐	☐	(10) Are the ideas written in complete sentences?
☐	☐	(11) Is there a variety of sentence structures?
☐	☐	(12) Do all the subjects and verbs agree?
☐	☐	(13) Are verbs in the correct tense?
☐	☐	(14) Are punctuation marks used correctly?
☐	☐	(15) Are words spelled correctly?
☐	☐	(16) Are capital letters used correctly?

Word Choice

☐	☐	(17) Is the use of words varied and appropriate?
☐	☐	(18) Are words used precisely?

Unit 4 Cumulative Review **Evaluating**

Because you cannot take an evaluation checklist with you to the GED essay test, it's a good idea to remember as many of the criteria as you can. Write the criteria you remember for each element below.

1. Response to the Prompt

_____

_____

_____

2. Organization

_____

_____

_____

_____

3. Development and Details

_____

_____

_____

4. Conventions of Edited American English

_____

_____

_____

_____

5. Word Choice

_____

_____

_____

Answers start on page 145.

Because you will have only 45 minutes to write your GED essay, you should try to spend only about five minutes evaluating your essay. If you need to take more time on this Mini-Test, you may, but keep in mind that you need to work on completing your evaluation in five minutes.

Refer to the first draft that you wrote for the following topic from page 57. Evaluate your draft. Make notes on it that show areas where it could be improved or corrected.

TOPIC

Is life better in a city or in a small town?

Explain your point of view in an essay. Use your personal observations, experience, and knowledge to support your view.

Think About POWER Step 4 ....

When you have finished evaluating your essay on the topic above, answer these questions.

1. Which items on the checklist match your notes about areas of your essay to be corrected or improved?

2. Which criteria (if any) are not clear to you, in terms of how to do your evaluation?

3. What can you do to find out more information about applying the criteria to your essay?

 Save your evaluation of this essay. If you like, put your work in your Writing Portfolio. You will use this material again in the Mini-Test at the end of the next unit.

• •

In Unit 5, you will learn how to revise your essay.

Answers start on page 145.

UNIT 5

Revising

In your personal and work-related writing, you should revise your work to improve its clarity and organization. You also need to edit for correct sentence structure, grammar, capitalization, spelling, and punctuation. Then you can write a second draft incorporating your revisions.

On the GED essay, you will have 45 minutes to plan, write, and revise your essay. You will not have time to write a second draft, but you need to leave some time to review your work and make revisions. That is why the next step in the POWER writing process is revising. In this unit, you will learn to revise the presentation of your ideas and improve the organization of your essay. You will also learn how to proofread your writing for correct sentence structure, grammar, punctuation, and capitalization.

Revising your work is a chance to make it better.

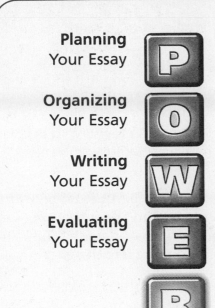

Planning Your Essay

Organizing Your Essay

Writing Your Essay

Evaluating Your Essay

Revising Your Essay

- Revising Ideas and Organization
- Editing for the Conventions of English

The lessons in this unit include:

Lesson 16:   Revising Ideas and Organization
Revising the organization and development of ideas in your essay will help you make it strong and effective.

Lesson 17:   Editing for the Conventions of English
In addition to revising, it is important to edit your essay for complete sentences, correct grammar, punctuation, spelling, and effective word choice.

Lesson 16

GED SKILL **Revising Ideas and Organization**

When you evaluate your essay (POWER Step 4), you identify areas that need strengthening or correcting. When you revise your essay (POWER Step 5), you decide how to change those areas and then make the changes.

Because evaluation is a two-step process, it is best to also revise in two steps. First, evaluate and revise your ideas and organization. Then evaluate and revise your use of the conventions of English. This second step of revision is sometimes called **proofreading.**

When you evaluated your presentation of ideas, you asked yourself three groups of questions:

Yes	No	**Response to the Prompt**
☐	☐	(1) Is there a clear main idea?
☐	☐	(2) Does the essay stick to the topic?

		Organization
☐	☐	(3) Does the introductory paragraph include a thesis statement and a preview?
☐	☐	(4) Does each body paragraph have a topic sentence and details related to the topic sentence?
☐	☐	(5) Does the concluding paragraph restate the thesis statement and review the ideas?
☐	☐	(6) Are there smooth transitions between paragraphs and between sentences?

		Development and Details
☐	☐	(7) Do the paragraphs include specific details and examples that support the topic sentences?
☐	☐	(8) Does the essay support the thesis statement?
☐	☐	(9) Is the essay free of irrelevant details?

TIP

You can revise your essay at any time. For example, correct a misspelled word or punctuation error when you first notice it. But do not spend too much time correcting until you have written your first draft.

Your answers to the questions tell you which parts of your essay need revising. For example, if your answer to question 3 is *no*, decide how to add a thesis statement for the essay topic. Use revision marks to add sentences. If your answer to question 9 is *no*, decide which sentences or phrases discuss things not directly related to the topic. Then cross them out.

Look at how one writer revised her essay on the topic assignment "State whether you think it is better to stay in one place or to move often and live in different places."

Note that the writer used some of these revision methods:
- Make corrections or add ideas between the lines or in the margin.
- Use a caret (^) to show where additions belong.
- Cross out any unwanted words or phrases.
- Rewrite any part that is illegible or too messy to read.

Main idea: It's better to live in different places than to stay in just one place.

Many people live in one place their entire lives and enjoy it, but I prefer experiencing different places. Living in one place provides security, but there are many disadvantages to this lifestyle. Living in new places is exciting and educationel.

Living in one place for a long time does have some advantages. You know where everything is and have the security of a routine. If you need help, you can ask a friend or neighbor. ^It is easy to cash checks and conduct other business because everyone knows you.

For me these advantages are overshadowed by the disadvantages of staying in one place. A comfortable routine can easily turn into a rut. You see the same people and do the same things over and over, and for me that means boredom! ^Finally, You never get exposed to fresh ideas and new ways of thinking. you begin to have a narrow concept of what the world is like.

Moving to a different city or town is an adventure. Everything will be unfamiliar to you. You will have new experiences you will have different things to see and do. Maybe you will be near mountains or by the ocean. You could learn to ski or surf. ~~But remember, long distance phone calls are expensive.~~ *Moving can give you opportunities you didn't have before. Best of all, you will be able to meet many people and make many new friends.*

So brave! Find a place you think you'd like, then pack up and move. Decide if you will move yourself or if you will hire a moving company. You'll have many more exciting experiences than people who stay in one place all their lives.

When the writer began evaluating her essay, she looked for ideas that did not relate to that main idea. She found a sentence in the fourth paragraph that did not seem to fit, so she crossed it out.

Then she looked at the ideas she had gathered and organized in POWER Steps 1 and 2. She added a sentence to the second paragraph about the advantage of cashing checks. Next, she thought of another supporting detail and added a sentence about getting exposed to new ideas to her third paragraph.

Evaluate the last paragraph of the essay again, using the checklist on page 80. Find another revision that could be made.

You should have crossed out *Decide if you will move yourself or if you will hire a moving company.* It does not relate to the topic of the paragraph.

TIP

When you revise your essay, compare it with your planning list of ideas. That will help you determine if you included all your ideas.

Read the following essay about the advantages and disadvantages of owning an automobile. Evaluate the essay for its presentation of ideas and then revise. Use the checklist on page 80 if you need to. Make your revisions directly on the essay.

Millions of people own automobiles. Sometimes they like owning their cars. Other times they don't. As every car owner knows, there are distinct advantages and disadvantages to owning an automobile. I own a car and so does my brother.

Owning a car offers several important practical advantages. A car provides easy transportation right from your home. You don't have to worry about bus routes or waiting for buses. Also, you can carry more things than you can carry on a bus.

Still another advantage to having a car is that it's fun. You can have a sound system in your car to listen to music. My favorite is country music. Driving along with the windows open and good music playing makes you feel alive.

While owning a car has advantages, it also has disadvantages. You have to get a driver's license. There is a test for this, and it can be difficult to pass. You also need car insurance, which costs money. The upkeep and gas for your car cost money, too. Sometimes you have to leave your car for repairs. This costs time and money.

Even though owning a car can cost you time and money, the advantages of owning a car outweigh these disadvantages. Bus riding is okay. My brother and I rode the bus everywhere before we got our cars. For convenience, fun, and carrying capacity, an automobile is a must.

Answers start on page 145.

GED SKILL **Editing for the Conventions of English**

After you make revisions to the ideas and organization of your essay, you should evaluate your use of the conventions of English and your choice of words and revise, if necessary. To evaluate (POWER Step 4), you asked yourself these two groups of questions:

Yes	No	**Conventions of Edited American English**
☐	☐	(10) Are the ideas written in complete sentences?
☐	☐	(11) Is there a variety of sentence structures?
☐	☐	(12) Do all the subjects and verbs agree?
☐	☐	(13) Are verbs in the correct tense?
☐	☐	(14) Are punctuation marks used correctly?
☐	☐	(15) Are words spelled correctly?
☐	☐	(16) Are capital letters used correctly?

Yes	No	**Word Choice**
☐	☐	(17) Is the use of words varied and appropriate?
☐	☐	(18) Are words used precisely?

Your answers to the questions tell you which corrections to make. For example, correct a sentence fragment by adding the necessary words and using a caret to show where they should be inserted. For a misspelled word, cross it out and write the correct spelling above it.

Look again at the essay about living in one place versus living in different places. The writer finished the second revision step and corrected her errors in the conventions of English. Her revision marks are in color.

Many people live in one place their entire lives and enjoy it, but I prefer experiencing different places. Living in one place provides security, but there are many disadvantages to this lifestyle. Living in new places is exciting and ~~educationel~~ educational.

Living in one place for a long time does have some advantages. You know where everything is and have the security of a routine. If you need help, you can ask a friend or neighbor. ∧ *It is easy to cash checks and conduct other business because everyone knows you.*

For me these advantages are overshadowed by the disadvantages of staying in one place. A comfortable routine can easily turn into a rut. You see the same people and do the same things over and over, and for me that means boredom! ^Finally, You never get exposed to fresh ideas and new ways of thinking. you begin to have a narrow concept of what the world is like.

Moving to a different city or town is an adventure. Everything will be unfamiliar to you. You will have new experiences. Y~~y~~ou will have different things to see and do. Maybe you will be near mountains or by the ocean. You could learn to ski or surf. ~~But remember, long distance phone calls are expensive.~~ Moving can give you opportunities you didn't have before. Best of all, you will be able to meet *a variety of* ~~many~~ people and make many new friends.

~~So brave!~~ Find a place you think you'd like, and then pack up and move. ~~Decide if you will move yourself or if you will hire a moving company.~~ You'll have many more exciting experiences than people who stay in one place all their lives.

The writer corrected a misspelled word in the first paragraph and a run-on sentence in the fourth paragraph. Then she realized she could improve her word choice in the last sentence of that paragraph by changing *many* to *a variety of*.

Use the checklist on page 84 to help you proofread for errors in the final paragraph. Revise if necessary.

You should have inserted the word *be* to correct the fragment at the beginning of the paragraph.

Be sure to use all the POWER steps when you write your GED essay. You may allow more or less time for a step than the time suggested, but following the steps will help you write a better essay.

Read the following essay on the popularity of fast-food restaurants. Edit the essay for its use of the conventions of English. Use a copy of the checklist on page 84 if you need to. Make your revisions directly on the essay.

Over the past few years, there has been an increase in the number of fast-food restaurants across the country. Its easy to see why. The increase is due to their convenience, their prices, and the rising number of families in which both husband and wife work outside the home.

Fast-food restaurants are conveniently located. They're built near companies, and along highways. In addition, they usually offer short menus you can make a quick, easy decision about what you want to order.

These restaurants also offer low prices. Hamburgers for a couple of dollars. Salad bars are usually inexpensive, too. Also, if you eat at a fast-food restaurant, you don't spend money on food at home or on the gas or electricity to cook it.

Finaly, more and more families is made up of working couples. The husband and wife are tired when they come home and don't want to cook they want to spend time with their kids. Therfore, they get everybody into the car and head out to the nearest fast-food restaurant.

The poplarity of fast food and the increase in restaurants serving it are easy to understand. These restaurants offer tired, hungry people just what they want.

Answers start on page 145.

Read the following essay about winning money in a lottery. Evaluate the essay for both its presentation of ideas and its use of the conventions of English and then revise. Use a copy of the checklists on pages 80 and 84 if you need to. Make your revisions directly on the essay.

I usually enter every contest or sweepstakes that come along, so I have given much thought to what I would do if I really won something big. I have decided that if I won the State lottery, I would help my family and the needy first, and then I will have some fun.

My family could use some financial help. I would love to pay off my parent's home so that they would never have another house payment to make. Financing a house is extremely expensive these days. I would put money aside for my sister's children to go to colege. In addition, I would buy my brother and his wife a car so that they wouldn't have to ride the bus to work.

I would also give money to needy causes that I think are important. For example, cancer and AIDS research.

With the rest of the money, I would have a great time. I would travel to places I have never been. Every time I go to the bookstore I see all these books about travel. I would never cook another meal I would eat out every day in a diffrent restaurant. I would hire a maid so that I would never have to clean the house again. Finally I would buy tickets to every concert, every sports event, and every new movie that comes to town.

Winning the lottery would be great for me and everyone else. Therefore, I will keep buying those lottery tickets

Answers start on page 146.

Unit 5 Cumulative Review **Revising**

Review your understanding of revising by answering the questions about the sample GED essay topic below.

TOPIC

Is life better in a city or in a small town?

Explain your point of view in an essay. Use your personal observations, experience, and knowledge to support your view.

---

1. Once you have written a first draft for this essay, what should you do next—evaluate and revise the ideas in your essay or evaluate and edit for the use of conventions of English? Why?

   _____

   _____

   _____

2. How can you make changes on your essay without rewriting it? List at least three methods.

   _____

   _____

   _____

   _____

   _____

3. How should you decide what to change?

   _____

   _____

   _____

4. How can you determine whether or not you included all the ideas you intended to include?

   _____

   _____

   _____

Answers start on page 146.

Because you will have only 45 minutes to write your GED essay, you should try to spend only about five minutes revising your essay. If you need to take more time on this Mini-Test, you may, but keep in mind that you need to work on completing your revision in five minutes.

Refer to your evaluation of the first draft of your essay on the following topic from page 77. Follow the steps you learned in this unit to revise your essay for presentation of ideas and conventions of English.

TOPIC

Is life better in a city or in a small town?

Explain your point of view in an essay. Use your personal observations, experience, and knowledge to support your view.

Think About POWER Step 5 ....

When you have finished revising your essay on the topic above, answer these questions.

1. Did you mark your changes neatly so that they can be easily read?

2. Was it easy or difficult to decide which revisions to make?

3. Some people make a list of errors that they make frequently. When they edit, they concentrate on those errors. Do you think this method would help you?

 Save your revision of your essay. If you like, put your work in your Writing Portfolio.

If you would like some additional tips on revising a first draft, be sure to read Unit 7, "Raising Your Score."

• •

In Unit 6, you will learn other methods for planning and organizing your essay.

Answers start on page 146.

UNIT 6

Varying Prewriting Techniques

Now that you have learned the basics of the POWER writing process, you are ready to perfect your approach to essay writing. One key to success is to find the techniques for planning and organizing that work best for you. In Unit 1, you practiced listing your ideas and making idea maps as a way to plan your essay. In Unit 2, you learned methods for grouping and labeling your ideas and expanding your groups. In this unit you will learn some other prewriting techniques.

While you are practicing for the GED essay, try out the different approaches to prewriting. Some will work better for you than others. Decide which technique works best for you, and plan to use it on the GED Test. This will make your prewriting work go smoothly and will give you enough time to draft and revise your essay.

Brainstorming and asking questions are good ways to come up with ideas.

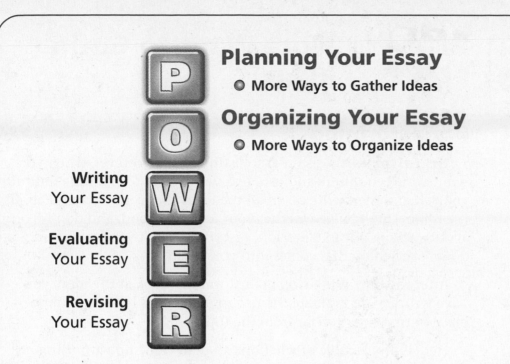

Planning Your Essay
- More Ways to Gather Ideas

Organizing Your Essay
- More Ways to Organize Ideas

Writing Your Essay

Evaluating Your Essay

Revising Your Essay

The lessons in this unit include:

Lesson 18: **More Ways to Gather Ideas**
Brainstorming, asking questions, and using idea circles are additional ways to gather ideas for your essay.

Lesson 19: **More Ways to Organize Ideas**
Once you have gathered ideas, you need to organize them. An idea map is a visual way to show the relationship between ideas. An outline is another organizing tool that helps you put your ideas in order.

GED SKILL More Ways to Gather Ideas

Brainstorming

brainstorming
gathering ideas by writing down all the thoughts that come into your head without judging them

Brainstorming is similar to listing ideas. However, when you brainstorm, you think and list ideas very quickly. Set a time limit for yourself and then write down all the ideas that come to mind about the topic. Don't judge whether your ideas are good, and don't worry about spelling or capitalization. Just think about your topic and write down everything that comes into your head.

After the time is up, stop brainstorming. Look at the ideas you have written and evaluate them. Cross out ideas that seem out of place or that stray too far from the topic.

Here is an example of what one student came up with using brainstorming. Read his list for the topic assignment "Why do so many people have pets?"

for company

all different kinds of pets

most people have dogs or cats

something to take care of

love and be loved

lots of people are lonely

pet shows

win prizes

impress people

something to own

can have control over

easier than training kids

good for kids

teaches them responsibility

teaches them about birth and death

can hunt with

beagles are good birders

The ideas are about pets, but many don't focus on reasons for having a pet. The writer needs to evaluate his ideas and cross out any that are off topic.

GED SKILL FOCUS

On a separate sheet of paper, practice brainstorming on the following topic: "What are some ways to make money?"

a. Give yourself five minutes to brainstorm ideas.

b. List all the ideas that come to mind. Don't stop to think if the ideas are good or well-written.

c. At the end of five minutes, stop writing. Go back and cross out irrelevant or off-topic ideas.

Answers start on page 146.

Asking Questions

Another way to get ideas is to ask yourself questions about the topic—*who, what, where, when, why,* and *how.* You used this method to expand your groups of ideas in POWER Step 2. It is also a good technique to use when you are stuck and cannot think of any ideas. For example, look at these ideas for the topic assignment "How does the weather affect people?"

Who?   Everyone's affected. Young and old. Men and women. Me personally.

What?   Outdoor plans can be affected. Travel. Sports.

Where?   Every place has good and bad weather. Some places have mostly good weather.

When?   Wintertime especially bad. Spring and summer thunderstorms too.

Why?   Because weather's everywhere.

How?   Moods—People feel blue when it's rainy, good when it's warm and sunny. Kids can't play outside in bad weather. Heating and cooling bills.

TIP

You are more likely to get off topic when you brainstorm than when you carefully think of a list of ideas, so allow more time to decide which ideas to keep.

Not all the questions will relate to every topic. For example, answering *where* does not make sense if you are writing about the effects of watching TV because TV is almost everywhere. However, answering two or three of the questions will usually get some ideas rolling.

GED SKILL FOCUS

On a separate sheet of paper, answer these questions (*who, what, where, when, why, how*) about the following topic: **"What are some ways to spend money?"**

Answers start on page 146.

Using an Idea Circle

Still another way to get ideas is to use an idea circle.

idea circle
a diagram of nested circles that shows how widening groups of people are affected by something

An **idea circle** is a diagram of nested circles that shows how widening groups of people are affected by something. In the center ring, tell how a topic relates to you personally. In the middle ring, think about how it relates to the people around you— your family, relatives, friends, and co-workers—and write those ideas next. Finally, in the outer ring, think about how the topic relates to society at large and include those ideas.

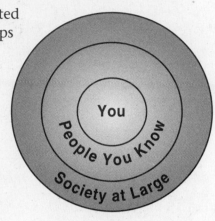

Read the ideas a student wrote using an idea circle for the topic assignment "What would life be like without television?"

For me: I probably watch too much anyway. Free me up to do other things. Work out. Spend time with my kids and wife. Talk to them, not just sit in front of the tube. Have real dinner conversation. Might try to go to a few baseball or football games.

For the people I know: Wife loves to watch news. Maybe she'd read newspaper? Kids watch too much now. They'd have to play games. Use their imagination.

For society: People wouldn't sit at home so much. Maybe go out to movies, restaurants. Probably better for the economy. Might even be friendlier to each other. Wouldn't feel so separate. If people are active, better for their health.

Unit 6: Varying Prewriting Techniques

Use the idea circle and the questions below to gather ideas that relate to the following topic: "How important is it for people to be satisfied with their jobs?"

1. How important is it for you to be satisfied with your job?

_____

_____

_____

_____

_____

2. How important is it for the people you know to be satisfied with their jobs?

_____

_____

_____

_____

_____

3. How important is it to society at large for people to be satisfied with their jobs?

_____

_____

_____

_____

_____

Answers start on page 146.

Lesson 19

GED SKILL More Ways to Organize Ideas

Mapping

mapping
a method of writing ideas to show the relationships between them

TIP

A map helps show how your groups of ideas relate to the main idea, but it does not show the order that the ideas will follow in your essay. After you map, number the groups to show the order you select.

Mapping is a visual way to show the relationships between ideas. To make a map, follow these steps:

1. Write your main idea in the middle of a piece of paper and circle it.
2. Write the label for an idea group, circle it, and connect it to the main idea.
3. List supporting ideas that belong with that group on lines extending from the circle.
4. Connect details and examples to the supporting ideas.
5. Continue with the next group until you map all your ideas.

When you finish mapping, you will have a diagram like the one below. Find the main idea in the middle and the supporting groups that surround it.

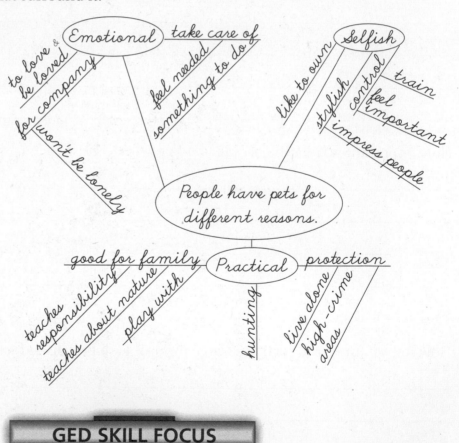

GED SKILL FOCUS

On a separate sheet of paper, map your ideas about ways to make money. Use the ideas you brainstormed on page 92. Follow the steps listed above. Use a copy of the blank idea map on page 128 if you prefer.

Answers start on page 146.

Outlining

outlining
creating an ordered list of ideas that shows how the ideas are related to each other

Outlining is a method of organizing by making an ordered list to show how ideas are related. To outline:

1. Use Roman numerals (I, II, III) to list the idea groups.
2. Use capital letters to list supporting ideas.
3. Use Arabic numerals (1, 2, 3) to list details and examples.

Here is an outline of the ideas mapped on page 96.

I. To Fill an Emotional Need
   A. For company so they won't be lonely
   B. To love and be loved
   C. Something to take care of
      1. Gives you something to do
      2. Makes you feel needed

II. For Practical Reasons
   A. Good for family to have pet
      1. Helps kids learn responsibility
      2. To play with
      3. Teaches about nature, birth, and death
   B. For protection
      1. People who live alone
      2. People who live in high-crime areas
   C. To hunt with

III. For Selfish Reasons
   A. Some people just like to own things
   B. Stylish thing to do — want to impress people
   C. Something to have control over
      1. Can train to obey on command
      2. Makes you feel important

GED SKILL FOCUS

On a separate sheet of paper, outline your ideas about job satisfaction. Use your ideas from the idea circle on page 95.

Answers start on page 146.

Unit 6 Cumulative Review Varying Prewriting Techniques

Review your understanding of prewriting—both gathering ideas and organizing them—by answering the questions about the sample GED essay assignment below.

TOPIC

Why do people follow fads? Are fads trivial, or do they serve a useful function?

Discuss your viewpoint in an essay. Use your personal observations, experience, and knowledge to support your view.

---

1. If you wanted to brainstorm about the topic, what would you do?

   _____

2. What should you do after you have brainstormed a list of ideas? Why?

   _____

   _____

3. What are the six questions that you can ask yourself to get ideas about the topic?

   _____

4. How would you use an idea circle to get ideas about the topic?

   _____

   _____

5. If you made an idea map for the topic, how would you show the main idea, supporting ideas, and details?

   _____

   _____

6. If you wrote an outline for the topic, how would you show the labels of the main idea groups, the supporting ideas, and details and examples?

   _____

   _____

Answers start on page 147.

Because you will have only 45 minutes to write your GED essay, try to spend about ten minutes prewriting it—five minutes gathering ideas and five minutes organizing the ideas. If you need to take more time on this Mini-Test, you may, but keep in mind that you need to work on prewriting for your essay in ten minutes.

Remember, at this point you are only gathering and organizing your ideas for this essay. You will continue to work on the essay in the next unit.

Read the essay topic below. Gather ideas on the topic by brainstorming, asking questions, or using an idea circle. Organize your ideas by mapping or outlining them.

TOPIC

Why do people follow fads? Are fads trivial, or do they serve a useful function?

Discuss your viewpoint in an essay. Use your personal observations, experience, and knowledge to support your view.

Think About Your Prewriting Techniques ....

When you have finished planning and organizing your ideas, answer the questions below.

1. Which prewriting technique did you use? Why did you choose that one?

2. Was it easy or difficult to think of enough ideas? If it was difficult, what technique might work better for you on the GED Test?

3. Which organizing technique did you use? Why did you choose that one?

4. Was it a good technique for this topic? Why or why not? If not, what technique might work better for you on the GED Test?

 Save your prewriting of your essay. If you like, put your work in your Writing Portfolio.

If you would like more practice with prewriting techniques, be sure to read Unit 8, "POWER Writing Review and Essay Strategy," and work with the additional GED topics on pages 126–127.

· ·

In Unit 7, you will learn ways to improve your score on your essay.

Answers start on page 147.

UNIT 7

Raising Your Score

Throughout this book, you have been learning how to use the POWER writing process. Through this process, you have learned how to plan, organize, write, edit, and revise an essay for the GED Language Arts, Writing Test.

Now that you have mastered the basics, you can work on improving your skills—and your score. This unit covers additional techniques that will create a positive impression of your writing skills in the mind of the essay readers. These techniques will help you to connect ideas logically, support your ideas convincingly, and use words descriptively.

Look for specific ways to improve your work.

100   **Unit 7: Raising Your Score**

Planning Your Essay

Organizing Your Essay

Evaluating Your Essay

Revising Your Essay

Writing Your Essay

- Using Transitions
- Providing Support with Facts and Opinions
- Using Precise Words

The lessons in this unit include:

Lesson 20: **Using Transitions**
One element of a good essay is strong organization. You can use transitions to show the relationship between ideas. Transitions can help your ideas flow from sentence to sentence and paragraph to paragraph.

Lesson 21: **Providing Support with Facts and Opinions**
You can strengthen your essay by providing examples, details, and opinions. These can be based on information from your personal experience or what you have read and heard from reliable sources. Your opinions on a topic can also be helpful, as long as you provide support for them as well.

Lesson 22: **Using Precise Words**
Your essay will be helped by expressing ideas clearly with precise words rather than general terms. Precise words, including action verbs and specific adjectives, give your reader a mental picture of your ideas and a better understanding of what you mean.

GED SKILL **Using Transitions**

In learning ways to organize your GED essay in Unit 2, you saw how a word or phrase can signal order of importance or compare-contrast. These words or phrases are called **transitions.** Transitions help connect one idea to the next. They can emphasize your organization and help make your ideas clear. When you use transitions, your ideas flow from one sentence to the next or from one paragraph to the next.

To see how transitions work, reread these paragraphs from the essay on seat belt laws in Unit 2. The paragraphs are organized according to order of importance. The transitions in color point out the order used and help show how the ideas are related.

transitions
words that make a smooth connection between ideas

TIP

If you forget to use transitions when you write your essay, you can add them when you evaluate and revise.

Seat belt laws are a source of money for cities. People ticketed for not wearing seat belts must pay fines, and this money can be used for roadway maintenance.

Even more important, seat belt laws improve traffic safety. Just by buckling up, people are reminded to drive more safely.

But the most important reason that seat belt laws are wise is that they save lives. Countless numbers of people are alive today because they were wearing their seat belts when they had an accident. Countless more have been saved from serious injury.

Reread the following paragraphs from the essay on watching television in Unit 2. The transitions in color use compare-contrast to help connect the ideas and show how they are alike and different.

There's no doubt that watching television can have positive effects. Adults can keep informed about current events by watching the evening news. They may even gain some practical knowledge about their health and other personal concerns. Children can learn from educational shows like *Sesame Street*. In addition, everyone can be entertained and even escape a little with cartoons, comedies, movies, and action shows.

On the other hand, watching television has some definite negative effects. Instead of just using it as a temporary escape, some people may watch television rather than deal with their problems. TV also keeps people from spending time with their family or from reading. In fact, it turns some people into couch potatoes, keeping them from any physical activity.

In addition, television gives people a false sense of what life is like. They see commercials on TV and feel they must have what's being advertised. They see violence on shows and think modern life is more violent than it really is, or they may even think it's all right to act violently.

As you can see in the essays and the chart below, you can use several kinds of transitions to tie ideas together.

To emphasize and connect	Use these transitions
1. ideas that are different (contrast)	• on one hand, although, instead, in spite of, in contrast, however, but, while, still, yet
2. ideas that are alike (compare)	• also, too, in addition, and
3. an example to a related idea	• for example, for instance, such as, like
4. a cause to an effect (cause-effect)	• because, so that, since, therefore, as a result
5. points you want to make	• in fact, indeed, moreover

Read the sentences below and underline the appropriate transitions.

Many people watch the shopping channel on TV, and (in contrast/ as a result), they buy things they don't need. (In addition/For instance), they pay more than they would have at a regular store.

In the first sentence, you were correct if you chose *as a result* because it shows the cause-effect relationship between watching the shopping channel and buying unnecessary items. In the second sentence, *in addition* shows that buying unneeded things and paying more are both negative effects of watching the shopping channel.

GED SKILL FOCUS

Read these paragraphs and underline the best transitions to show the connections between ideas.

Having more leisure time can have both good and bad effects on a person's life. (On one hand/ Therefore), more leisure time can improve the quality of many people's lives. They would have more time to spend with their families, to learn new things, to explore their creativity, and to travel. (On the other hand/As a result), family relationships would improve. (Instead/Additionally), people would become skilled in sports and hobbies.

(On the other hand/For example), too much leisure time can have some bad effects. People with little imagination or low self-esteem don't always do well with time on their hands. (In fact/So that), some people become depressed or bored. (However/Also), some join gangs or get into trouble with the law.

Answers start on page 147.

GED SKILL **Providing Support with Facts and Opinions**

In POWER Step 3, you learned to use details and examples to support your topic sentences. Another good way to add support in your essay is to use facts and opinions.

A **fact** is a statement that can be proved true. You can check a fact with a reliable source, such as a reference book. A fact in a GED essay does not have to be a statistic or a specific name or detail; it can be a general statement about the topic that you know to be true.

An **opinion** is a statement of preference or belief. Although someone can agree or disagree with it, an opinion cannot be proved true. When a GED essay asks for your opinion, you write about your beliefs and feelings. You might use words that make value judgments, such as *beautiful, best, worthless,* or *important.*

Read this paragraph about the problem of illegal drugs. It contains three details supporting the main idea that drugs are a serious problem.

> The drug problem has become serious. People are taking dangerous drugs, such as cocaine. They are also committing crimes to get money for drugs. In addition, some people are becoming drug dealers because of the money they can make.

Now read the paragraph with three facts and two opinions added to help support the main idea. The additional facts are in color, and the opinions are underlined.

> The drug problem has become serious. People are taking dangerous drugs, such as cocaine. They are also committing crimes to get money for drugs. Drug use and related crimes have risen over the years. In addition, some people are becoming drug dealers because of the money they can make. This is an alarming and sad situation. Every year, people lose their lives to drugs. Either they die of overdoses, or they die in violence connected to drugs. This tremendous waste of lives is senseless and shameful.

To think of facts to include in your essay, consider what you have heard and read about the topic—on the news; in newspapers, books, and magazines; or from other reliable sources. To think of opinions to include in your essay, consider what you believe and why you think as you do.

fact
a statement that can be proved true

opinion
a statement of preference or belief

TIP

It is not always necessary to begin an opinion with "I believe" or "I think" or "In my opinion." Just state your opinion clearly and forcefully.

Write *F* before the fact and *O* before the opinion.

_____ a. Drug users in public transportation, such as bus drivers and train engineers, have caused accidents and injuries.

_____ b. Drug abuse is the most important problem in our society.

You were correct if you wrote *F* before *option a* because the causes of accidents can be proven. *Option b* is an opinion because it is a judgment and uses the words *most important.*

GED SKILL FOCUS

A. Suppose you are writing an essay on the need for taxes. Write *F* before the facts you could use to support ideas about taxes. Write *O* before the opinions.

_____ 1. Polls show that many people want taxes to be changed.

_____ 2. People who believe taxes are too high are mistaken.

_____ 3. Taxes help provide aid for education and social programs.

_____ 4. There is no more important use for tax dollars than schools.

_____ 5. Tax dollars are used to build and maintain roads and bridges at the local, state, and national levels.

_____ 6. Thousands of people use the national parks every year.

_____ 7. The beauty of the national parks is worth the tax money spent on them.

B. Suppose you are writing an essay about ways to spend money on entertainment. For each supporting idea, write at least one fact and one opinion.

1. Movies

   Fact: _____

   Opinion: _____

2. Sports

   Fact: _____

   Opinion: _____

3. Hobbies

   Fact: _____

   Opinion: _____

Answers start on page 147.

Lesson 22

GED SKILL Using Precise Words

Clarity refers to how clearly you present the ideas in your essay. A good way to express ideas clearly is to use precise words rather than general terms. **Precise words** give your reader a mental picture of your ideas and a better understanding of what you mean. Precise language makes writing lively and interesting.

To understand how a few word changes can help the clarity of writing, read the paragraph below. Notice the general words in color.

> When you go for a job interview, your appearance tells your potential employer something about you. If you look nice, you give the impression that you are serious about work. If you look bad, it suggests you don't care about work. So wear good clothes, and remember that your appearance tells something about you even before you talk.

Now read the paragraph with precise words replacing the general terms. The precise words help you picture what the writer means.

> When you arrive for a job interview, your appearance tells your potential employer something about you. If you look neat and clean, you give the impression that you are serious about work. If you look sloppy or ungroomed, it suggests you don't care about work. So wear clean, pressed, businesslike clothes, and remember that your appearance reveals something about you even before you utter a word.

To help you think of precise words, use the following techniques:

- Picture in your mind what you want to discuss. Think of words that illustrate what you see.
- Ask yourself questions such as, *How does this look? sound? smell? feel? taste?* Use these sensory words in your descriptions.
- Visualize actions to help you find strong verbs like *claim, stroll,* and *crash* instead of *say, walk,* and *hit.*
- Think of words you have heard on the news, on the radio, in movies, or in your class. Think of words you have read.

Read the sentence below. Use one of the techniques discussed above to replace the underlined word with a more precise word.

The job offer made Gisela <u>happy</u>.

You could have substituted *overjoyed* or *elated* or *ecstatic* or many other precise words for *happy*.

precise words
specific, exact
language

TIP

If you can't think of a precise word when you write, use a general term. Replace it with a precise word when you evaluate and revise.

A. List precise words to describe each item. Answer the questions if you need help.

1. city traffic (What does it look like? sound like? smell like? How does it feel to be in it? What actions take place in traffic? How would a TV reporter describe traffic?)

   _____   _____

   _____   _____

   _____   _____

2. telephone (What does it sound like? How does using it make you feel? What actions take place while you use the telephone? How would a telephone be described in a book?)

   _____   _____

   _____   _____

   _____   _____

3. money (What does it feel like to touch it? How does it look? How does having it make you feel? not having it? What can it do for you? How do other people describe money?)

   _____   _____

   _____   _____

   _____   _____

4. summertime (How does it look? What are the smells, sounds, and tastes that go with it? What does it feel like? What actions take place in summertime? How is it described on the radio?)

   _____   _____

   _____   _____

   _____   _____

B. Write a more precise word (or words) to replace the underlined words.

1. Listening to music is <u>nice</u>. _____

2. Raising a child is <u>hard</u>. _____

3. Crime is a <u>big</u> problem. _____

Answers start on page 147.

Unit 7 Cumulative Review Raising Your Score

Review your understanding of techniques to raise your score by answering the questions about the sample GED essay assignment below.

TOPIC

Why do people follow fads? Are fads trivial, or do they serve a useful function?

Discuss your viewpoint in an essay. Use your personal observations, experience, and knowledge to support your view.

---

1. What is the purpose of transition words? _____
_____

2. What are some transition words you might use in an essay explaining the reasons people follow fads?
_____

3. What is the difference between a fact and an opinion? _____
_____
_____

4. How could you find facts for your essay on fads? _____
_____
_____

5. How could you find opinions for your essay on fads? _____
_____

6. Why are precise words better than general terms? _____
_____

7. What techniques could you use to help you think of precise words to include in your essay on fads?
_____
_____
_____

Answers start on page 148.

Because you will have only 45 minutes to write your GED essay, try to spend about 25 minutes writing the first draft, 5 minutes evaluating it, and 5 minutes revising it. If you need to take more time on this Mini-Test, you may, but keep in mind that you need to work on completing the first draft, evaluating, and revising in a total of 35 minutes.

Refer to the ideas that you organized on page 99 for the following topic. On a separate sheet of paper, follow the steps you learned in this unit to write a first draft for an essay on the topic.

TOPIC

Why do people follow fads? Are fads trivial, or do they serve a useful function?

Discuss your viewpoint in an essay. Use your personal observations, experience, and knowledge to support your view.

Think About Ways of Raising Your Score ·····················

When you have finished writing, evaluating, and revising, answer the questions below.

1. At which POWER stage is it easiest for you to insert transitions?

2. Was it easy or difficult to think of facts and opinions to support your essay? If it was difficult, what might work better for you on the GED Test?

3. Was it easy or difficult to think of precise words to clarify your writing? If it was difficult, what technique might work better for you on the GED Test?

 You may save your work in your Writing Portfolio.

If you would like more practice with raising your score, be sure to read Unit 8, "POWER Writing Review and Essay Strategy," and work with the additional essay topics on pages 126 and 127.

··

Answers start on page 148.

POWER Writing Review and Essay Strategy

This unit will enable you to put together all of the pieces of the POWER writing process and to practice writing an effective GED essay. You will review reading and analyzing the essay prompt, which presents the topic that you will be writing about. You will practice using the prewriting strategy that works best for you.

This unit will provide you with a variety of checklists that will help guide you in evaluating and revising your essay. You can actually read the scoring guide that will be used to evaluate your essay on the GED Test. Finally, you can take two simulated GED essay tests. If you feel you need even more practice, there are extra sample essay topics at the end of the unit.

Use everything you have learned to write an effective essay.

In this unit you will work on:

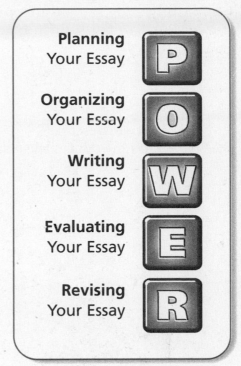

Planning
Your Essay

Organizing
Your Essay

Writing
Your Essay

Evaluating
Your Essay

Revising
Your Essay

The Five-Paragraph Essay
A good way to respond to a GED topic is to write a five-paragraph essay, including an introduction, body, and conclusion.

The POWER Writing Process
This process helps you to write an effective essay in five main steps: planning, organizing, writing, evaluating, and revising.

Prewriting
Prewriting is another name for the planning and organizing stages of the POWER writing process.

Writing: Organization, Support, and Clarity
As you are writing your essay, keep your ideas organized, provide support through examples and details, and be clear and to the point.

Evaluating and Revising
When you evaluate your essay, review how well you responded to the prompt; how you developed, organized and supported your ideas; and how you correctly used words, spelling, punctuation, grammar, and capitalization.

Scoring an Essay
You can review the scoring guide that readers will use to assign a score to your GED essay.

Your Personal Writing Strategy
You can customize the POWER writing process to your own personal writing style and preferences.

Simulated Test A and Simulated Test B
These two simulated tests will allow you to practice for the GED essay.

Additional Essay Topics
Nine more topics provide additional practice in writing an essay.

The Five-Paragraph Essay

Remember that a good way to respond to a GED topic assignment is to write a five-paragraph essay. The five paragraphs make up three distinct parts of the essay. The three parts serve different purposes.

Introduction
One paragraph introduces the essay.

> **Thesis statement** tells the main idea of the entire essay.
> **Preview sentences** tell the approach to the topic.
> **Background sentences** may be included to give information about the topic.

Body
Three paragraphs develop the topic by supporting the thesis statement.

> **Body Paragraph 1**
> **Topic sentence** tells the paragraph's main idea.
> **Supporting sentences** give details, examples, facts, and opinions about the topic sentence.

> **Body Paragraph 2**
> **Topic sentence** tells the paragraph's main idea.
> **Supporting sentences** give details, examples, facts, and opinions about the topic sentence.

> **Body Paragraph 3**
> **Topic sentence** tells the paragraph's main idea.
> **Supporting sentences** give details, examples, facts, and opinions about the topic sentence.

Conclusion
One paragraph wraps up the essay.

> **Restates** the thesis statement.
> **Reviews** the main support.

The POWER Writing Process

Remember that writing an effective essay takes five main steps.

    Step 1 **P**lanning
    Step 2 **O**rganizing
    Step 3 **W**riting
    Step 4 **E**valuating
    Step 5 **R**evising

Each of the five steps incorporates smaller steps.

Step 1   **PLANNING** your essay involves:
- Understanding the writing assignment
- Gathering your ideas—using techniques such as listing, mapping, brainstorming, or making idea circles to get ideas
- Choosing your main idea

Step 2   **ORGANIZING** your essay involves:
- Grouping and labeling your ideas—using techniques such as circling and labeling in groups, mapping, and outlining
- Expanding your groups
- Ordering your groups

Step 3   **WRITING** your essay involves:
- Writing your introductory paragraph
- Writing your body paragraphs
- Writing your concluding paragraph

Step 4   **EVALUATING** your essay involves:
- Evaluating your ideas and organization
- Evaluating your use of the conventions of English

Step 5   **REVISING** your essay involves:
- Revising your ideas and organization
- Revising your use of the conventions of English

TIP

Write using the POWER steps as often as possible so the process becomes automatic. Then, when you take the GED Essay Test, you'll remember the five steps and will be able to follow them in order.

Prewriting

Prewriting involves the **planning** and **organizing** stages of the POWER writing process.

Planning includes relying on key words in the instructions to understand what you should write about.

planning
- understanding the writing assignment
- gathering your ideas
- choosing your main idea

If the instructions say	You should
explain why state the reasons	write about causes or reasons
explain the effects discuss the advantages and disadvantages	write about effects
describe	discuss the qualities of something
state your position present your view	tell what you think about an issue and why
discuss the similarities and differences compare and contrast	explain how things are alike and different

organizing
- grouping and labeling your ideas
- expanding your groups
- ordering your groups

Organizing includes putting your groups of ideas in a logical order.

If you are writing about	Try using
reasons or causes good or bad effects the qualities of one thing how you feel about an issue	order of importance
good and bad effects advantages and disadvantages	contrast
the qualities of two things	compare and contrast

GED SKILL FOCUS

Complete the planning and organizing steps for the essay topic below.

TOPIC

"Nice guys finish last." Do you agree or disagree with that saying?

Explain your point of view in an essay.

Answers start on page 148.

Writing: Organization, Support, and Clarity

writing
- writing your introductory paragraph
- writing your body paragraphs
- writing your concluding paragraph

TIP

Leave wide margins on your paper so that you can add ideas when you revise. Leave space between the lines to correct errors.

When **writing** your essay, a good way to strengthen the organization and clarity of your essay is to use transitions. Transitions show the connections between ideas. Transitions at the beginning of paragraphs help indicate how your essay is organized.

If the organization of ideas is	Use these transitions
1. order of importance *(Discuss why you think . . .)*	• more important, most important, better, best, first, second, last
2. compare *(Explain how they are alike . . .)*	• like, also, similarly, in the same way
3. contrast *(Describe the good and bad effects . . .)*	• on the other hand, in contrast, however, but, whereas, while, rather than, instead

You also want to use transitions to connect ideas within a paragraph and show how they are related.

To emphasize and connect	Use these transitions
1. an example to a related idea	• for example, for instance, such as, like
2. ideas that are alike	• also, too, in addition, and
3. a cause to its related effect	• because, since, therefore, as a result
4. points you are making	• in fact, indeed, moreover
5. a sequence of events	• first, next, then, finally

To add support to your essay, include facts and opinions. Use what you have heard and read about the topic. Use what you believe and feel about the topic.

To make your ideas clear to your reader, include precise words.
- Use sensory words that describe how things feel, sound, smell, look, or taste.
- Picture the ideas in your head and describe exactly what you see.
- Ask yourself questions to help you come up with precise words.

GED SKILL FOCUS

Write the essay that you planned and organized for the GED Skill Focus on page 114.

Answers start on page 148.

Evaluating and Revising

When **evaluating** and **revising** the presentation of ideas in your essay, first consider these three areas—your response to the prompt, organization, and development and details. Then consider your use of the conventions of English and word choice.

evaluating
- evaluating your ideas and organization
- evaluating your use of the conventions of English

revising
- revising your ideas and organization
- revising your use of the conventions of English

Yes	No	**Response to the Prompt**
☐	☐	(1) Is there a clear main idea?
☐	☐	(2) Does the essay stick to the topic?

Organization

☐	☐	(3) Does the introductory paragraph include a thesis statement and a preview?
☐	☐	(4) Does each body paragraph have a topic sentence and details related to the topic sentence?
☐	☐	(5) Does the concluding paragraph restate the thesis statement and review the ideas?
☐	☐	(6) Are there smooth transitions between paragraphs and between sentences?

Development and Details

☐	☐	(7) Do the paragraphs include specific details and examples that support the topic sentences?
☐	☐	(8) Does the essay support the thesis statement?
☐	☐	(9) Is the essay free of irrelevant details?

Conventions of Standard Written English

☐	☐	(10) Are the ideas written in complete sentences?
☐	☐	(11) Is there a variety of sentence structures?
☐	☐	(12) Do all the subjects and verbs agree?
☐	☐	(13) Are verbs in the correct tense?
☐	☐	(14) Are punctuation marks used correctly?
☐	☐	(15) Are words spelled correctly?
☐	☐	(16) Are capital letters used correctly?

Word Choice

☐	☐	(17) Is the use of words varied and appropriate?
☐	☐	(18) Are words used precisely?

GED SKILL FOCUS

Evaluate and revise the essay that you wrote for the GED Skill Focus on page 115. Then, review the GED Essay Scoring Guide on page 117. Read and score the essay you evaluated and revised for this GED Skill Focus.

Answers start on page 148.

Scoring an Essay

		1 Inadequate	2 Marginal	3 Adequate	4 Effective
Response to the Prompt		Reader has difficulty identifying or following the writer's ideas.	Reader occasionally has difficulty understanding or following the writer's ideas.	Reader understands writer's ideas.	Reader understands and easily follows the writer's expression of ideas.
		Attempts to address prompt but with little or no success in establishing a focus.	Addresses the prompt, though the focus may shift.	Uses the writing prompt to establish a main idea.	Presents a clearly focused main idea that addresses the prompt.
Organization		Fails to organize ideas.	Shows some evidence of organizational plan.	Uses an identifiable organizational plan.	Establishes a clear and logical organization.
Development and Details		Demonstrates little or no development; usually lacks details or examples or presents irrelevant information.	Has some development but lacks specific details; may be limited to a listing, repetitions, or generalizations.	Has focused but occasionally uneven development; incorporates some specific detail.	Achieves coherent development with specific and relevant details and examples.
Conventions of EAE		Exhibits minimal or no control of sentence structure and the conventions of EAE.	Demonstrates inconsistent control of sentence structure and the conventions of EAE.	Generally controls sentence structure and the conventions of EAE.	Consistently controls sentence structure and the conventions of Edited American English (EAE).
Word Choice		Exhibits weak and/or inappropriate words.	Exhibits a narrow range of word choice, often including inappropriate selections.	Exhibits appropriate word choice.	Exhibits varied and precise word choice.

Reprinted with permission of the American Council on Education.

Your Personal Writing Strategy

You have learned several techniques to help you follow the POWER writing process. Different techniques are presented because every writer is different. To write your best GED essay, you need to determine the techniques that work best for you. Then you can create your own writing strategy for scoring high on the GED essay.

As you answer the questions below, use your responses to the questions at the end of the Mini-Tests in this book. They will help you decide on the best strategy for you at each step in the process.

Gathering Ideas

Which of these techniques was most useful for you in gathering ideas? Which seemed the second best way? Number the techniques below 1 and 2. Then write your choices in the chart on page 120.

_____ making a list

_____ drawing an idea map

_____ brainstorming

_____ asking questions

_____ using an idea circle

Organizing Ideas

Which of these techniques was most helpful to you in grouping and ordering ideas? Write it in the chart on page 120.

_____ circling and labeling in groups on the list

_____ rewriting the ideas in lists; labeling the lists

_____ drawing an idea map

_____ outlining

Writing

Which of these tips do you have the most trouble remembering? Write them in the chart on page 120.

_____ stick to your organization plan

_____ add more ideas to the first ones I write down

_____ write neatly and legibly

_____ leave space between lines and in the margins for corrections

© 2002 Steck-Vaughn Company. GED Essay. Permission granted to reproduce for classroom use.

Evaluating and Revising

Which of these areas do you need to pay attention to when you evaluate and revise? Check any that you want to be sure to remember. Write them in the chart on page 120.

Presentation of Ideas

_____ stating the thesis clearly in the introductory paragraph

_____ writing preview sentences in the introductory paragraph

_____ sticking to the topic

_____ writing topic sentences for each body paragraph

_____ including details, examples, facts, and opinions as support

_____ expressing ideas clearly with precise words and transitions

_____ restating the topic in the concluding paragraph

_____ reviewing the ideas in the concluding paragraph

Conventions of English

_____ using correct sentence structure

_____ using a variety of sentence structures

_____ making sure that subjects and verbs agree

_____ making sure that verbs are in the correct tense and form

_____ checking the punctuation

_____ looking over the spelling

_____ checking the capitalization

_____ checking word choice

Using Your Time

Each of the five POWER steps takes a certain amount of time. This chart suggests an appropriate amount of time to spend on each step:

Planning:	5 minutes	
Organizing:	5 minutes	
Writing:	25 minutes	45 minutes total
Evaluating:	5 minutes	
Revising:	5 minutes	

However, the time frame that works best for you may be different. Perhaps you need less time to think of ideas but more time to organize them. Or you may need less time to write your essay and more time to revise it. Write the times you think you need to spend on each step of the writing process in the chart on page 120.

My Writing Strategy	Time
Planning The technique I will use to gather ideas is _____ _____ . If I have trouble thinking of ideas, I'll also try _____ _____ .	____ min.
Organizing The technique I will use to group and order my ideas is _____ _____ _____ _____ .	____ min.
Writing I will follow my organizational plan to write an introductory paragraph, three body paragraphs, and a concluding paragraph. When I write, I'll make sure I _____ _____ _____ .	____ min.
Evaluating and Revising My Presentation of Ideas I will pay close attention to these areas when I evaluate and revise: _____ _____ _____	____ min.
Evaluating and Revising the Conventions of English I will pay close attention to these areas when I evaluate and revise: _____ _____ _____	____ min. **Total 45 min.**

Put your essay-writing strategy to the test. Follow the POWER writing steps and your writing strategy to write an essay for the topic assignment below. Use a copy of the Answer Sheet on pages 156 and 157 or your own paper. Time yourself on each step. Work for no more than 45 minutes.

TOPIC

Why do some people prefer to watch television rather than read books, newspapers, and magazines?

Give your reasons in an essay. Use your personal observations, experience, and knowledge to support them.

After you have written your essay, check your writing strategy. Change any technique or problem area you feel you need to.

Check the times you listed on your strategy for each step. Decide if you accomplished everything you needed to do in that amount of time. If not, go back and adjust the times on your writing strategy.

Answers start on page 148.

**Language Arts,
Writing, Part II**

Essay Directions and Topic

Look at the box on the next page. In the box are your assigned topic and the letter of that topic.

You must write on the assigned topic ONLY.

You will have 45 minutes to write on your assigned essay topic. You may return to the multiple-choice section after you complete your essay if you have time remaining in this test period. Do not return the Language Arts, Writing booklet until you finish both Parts I and II of the Language Arts, Writing Test.

Two evaluators will score your essay according to its overall effectiveness. Their evaluation will be based on the following features:

- Well-focused main points
- Clear organization
- Specific development of your ideas
- Control of sentence structure, punctuation, grammar, word choice, and spelling

REMEMBER, YOU MUST COMPLETE BOTH THE MULTIPLE-CHOICE QUESTIONS (PART I) AND THE ESSAY (PART II) TO RECEIVE A SCORE ON THE LANGUAGE ARTS, WRITING TEST. To avoid having to repeat both parts of the test, be sure to do the following:

- Do not leave the pages blank.
- Write legibly in ink so that the evaluators will be able to read your writing.
- Write on the assigned topic. If you write on a topic other than the one assigned, you will not receive a score for the Language Arts, Writing Test.
- Write your essay on the lined pages of the separate answer sheet on pages 156–157 of this book. Only the writing on these pages will be scored.

TOPIC A

What are the advantages and disadvantages of a "child-free" lifestyle?

In your essay, explore the advantages and disadvantages of choosing not to have children.

Part II is a test to determine how well you can use written language to explain your ideas.

In preparing your essay, you should take the following steps:

- Read the **DIRECTIONS** and the **TOPIC** carefully.
- Plan your essay before you write. Use the scratch paper provided to make any notes. These notes will be collected but not scored.
- Before you turn in your essay, reread what you have written and make any changes that will improve your essay.

Your essay should be long enough to develop the topic adequately.

Answers start on page 148.

Language Arts,
Writing, Part II

Essay Directions and Topic

Look at the box on the next page. In the box are your assigned topic and the letter of that topic.

You must write on the assigned topic ONLY.

You will have 45 minutes to write on your assigned essay topic. You may return to the multiple-choice section after you complete your essay if you have time remaining in this test period. Do not return the Language Arts, Writing booklet until you finish both Parts I and II of the Language Arts, Writing Test.

Two evaluators will score your essay according to its overall effectiveness. Their evaluation will be based on the following features:

- Well-focused main points
- Clear organization
- Specific development of your ideas
- Control of sentence structure, punctuation, grammar, word choice, and spelling

REMEMBER, YOU MUST COMPLETE BOTH THE MULTIPLE-CHOICE QUESTIONS (PART I) AND THE ESSAY (PART II) TO RECEIVE A SCORE ON THE LANGUAGE ARTS, WRITING TEST. To avoid having to repeat both parts of the test, be sure to do the following:

- Do not leave the pages blank.
- Write legibly <u>in ink</u> so that the evaluators will be able to read your writing.
- Write on the assigned topic. If you write on a topic other than the one assigned, you will not receive a score for the Language Arts, Writing Test.
- Write your essay on the lined pages of the separate answer sheet on pages 156–157 of this book. Only the writing on these pages will be scored.

```
┌─────────────────────────────────────────────────────────────────┐
│                          TOPIC B                                 │
│                                                                  │
│   Why do many people love to watch sports?                       │
│                                                                  │
│   Write an essay explaining the reasons.                         │
│                                                                  │
│                                                                  │
└─────────────────────────────────────────────────────────────────┘
```

Part II is a test to determine how well you can use written language to explain your ideas.

In preparing your essay, you should take the following steps:

- Read the **DIRECTIONS** and the **TOPIC** carefully.
- Plan your essay before you write. Use the scratch paper provided to make any notes. These notes will be collected but not scored.
- Before you turn in your essay, reread what you have written and make any changes that will improve your essay.

Your essay should be long enough to develop the topic adequately.

Answers start on page 148.

Additional Essay Topics

Use these topics to gain additional experience writing GED essays. Use your personal test-taking strategy to follow all the POWER Steps. Take no more than 45 minutes to write each essay.

TOPIC 1

Describe the ways in which computers have affected our lives.

In your essay, you may wish to deal with the good effects, the bad effects, or both.

TOPIC 2

What are some tips for saving money?

In your essay, offer advice on stretching an income. You may want to include both "dos" and "don'ts."

TOPIC 3

How do pop music and culture affect young people in our society?

In your essay, describe the impact of popular music on young people. You may deal with the good effects, the bad effects, or both.

TOPIC 4

Compare and contrast the person you are now with the person you were five or ten years ago.

In your essay, explain how you have changed.

TOPIC 5

How are people affected by constantly seeing ads in magazines and newspapers and on TV and radio?

Write an essay stating the effects of ads on the buying public.

TOPIC 6

Why do people continue doing things that are bad for them, even when there is clear evidence that these activities are harmful?

In your essay, give reasons for this behavior.

TOPIC 7

In what one way would you like to improve your life?

In your essay, identify the way you would improve. Explain the reasons for your choice.

TOPIC 8

What does one need to consider when choosing a job, besides the work one will be doing?

In your essay, describe the considerations that impact job choice. Explain the considerations.

TOPIC 9

Why do many people buy state lottery tickets, even though they have very little chance of winning?

State the reasons for high lottery sales.

Answers start on page 148.

Idea Map Form

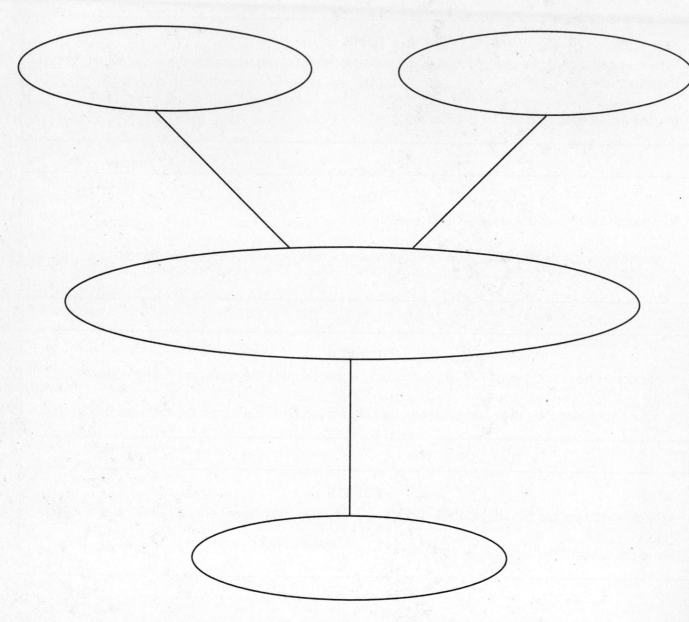

Evaluation Checklist

Yes	No	**Response to the Prompt**
☐	☐	(1) Is there a clear main idea?
☐	☐	(2) Does the essay stick to the topic?

Organization

Yes	No	
☐	☐	(3) Does the introductory paragraph include a thesis statement and a preview?
☐	☐	(4) Does each body paragraph have a topic sentence and details related to the topic sentence?
☐	☐	(5) Does the concluding paragraph restate the thesis statement and review the ideas?
☐	☐	(6) Are there smooth transitions between paragraphs and between sentences?

Development and Details

Yes	No	
☐	☐	(7) Do the paragraphs include specific details and examples that support the topic sentences?
☐	☐	(8) Does the essay support the thesis statement?
☐	☐	(9) Is the essay free of irrelevant details?

Conventions of Standard Written English

Yes	No	
☐	☐	(10) Are the ideas written in complete sentences?
☐	☐	(11) Is there a variety of sentence structures?
☐	☐	(12) Do all the subjects and verbs agree?
☐	☐	(13) Are verbs in the correct tense?
☐	☐	(14) Are punctuation marks used correctly?
☐	☐	(15) Are words spelled correctly?
☐	☐	(16) Are capital letters used correctly?

Word Choice

Yes	No	
☐	☐	(17) Is the use of words varied and appropriate?
☐	☐	(18) Are words used precisely?

Revision Methods

- Cross out any unwanted words or phrases.
- Make corrections or add ideas between the lines or in the margin.
- Use a caret (^) to show where additions belong.
- Rewrite any part that is illegible or too messy to read.

Sentence Structure

Varying Sentence Structures

There are three different kinds of sentences: simple, compound, and complex. Use a variety of sentence structures to make your writing interesting.

A **simple sentence** contains a subject and a verb and expresses a complete thought. It is an **independent clause.** In these examples, the subject is underlined once and the verb twice.

Children eat ice cream. In fact, people of all ages love it.

A **compound sentence** is formed by combining two simple sentences, or independent clauses, with a connector or a semicolon. The connector shows the relationship between the clauses. The connector may be a coordinating conjunction or a conjunctive adverb.

Coordinating conjunction (requires a comma)
Simple: Alice has a talent for singing. She joined a chorus.
Compound: Alice has a talent for singing, so she joined a chorus.

Conjunctive adverb (requires a semicolon and comma)
Simple: Her sister has a bad voice. She got into the chorus anyway.
Compound: Her sister has a bad voice; however, she got into the chorus anyway.

Semicolon alone
Simple: Young musicians work very hard. Their social life suffers.
Compound: Young musicians work very hard; their social life suffers.

A **complex sentence** is formed by joining an independent clause with a dependent, or subordinate, clause. The subordinate clause has a subject and verb but is not a complete thought. In a complex sentence, the subordinate clause adds details to the main independent clause.

Subordinate clause: So that he can earn money for music lessons.
Complex sentence: Dennis is going to change jobs so that he can earn money for music lessons.

Another way to make your writing more interesting is by combining details from separate sentences into one sentence.

Separate: Dennis plays the guitar. He also plays the mandolin. He recently took up the viola.
Combined: Dennis plays the guitar, mandolin, and viola.

A. Combine each pair of sentences in two different ways. Use both complex and compound sentences.

1. Many people ride bicycles. They are a cheap, energy-saving alternative to cars.

   a. _____

   b. _____

2. Riding a bicycle is good exercise. Some people take up bicycle riding to lose weight.

   a. _____

   b. _____

3. In Holland, there are bicycle lanes on many streets. In the United States, bicycle lanes are more rare.

   a. _____

   b. _____

4. Children learn to ride a tricycle first. They may ride a bike with training wheels.

   a. _____

   b. _____

B. Rewrite the paragraph below, combining the sentences. Use both compound and complex sentences.

Few people take a cross-country trip by train these days. In the past, it was a common mode of transportation. A trip from Chicago to Seattle takes two and a half days. It is well worth it. On the journey, you pass through several mountain ranges. You also pass through many picturesque towns. You may not get much sleep. You have to sit up the whole time. You can get a sleeper car. There are a lot of interesting people to meet. You'll be distracted from your fatigue.

_____

_____

_____

_____

_____

_____

Answers start on page 148.

Fragments and Run-Ons

Fragments and run-ons are errors in sentence structure. A **fragment** does not express a complete thought. To fix a fragment, add words to complete the thought.

Fragment: The movie at the Odeon.
Sentence: The movie at the Odeon is supposed to be very good.

A **run-on sentence** combines two complete thoughts without correct punctuation or a connector. To fix a run-on, add correct punctuation and/or a connector.

Run-on: Last night we saw an old Robert Redford <u>film it</u> was great.
Run-on: Last night we saw an old Robert Redford <u>film, it</u> was great.
Correct: Last night we saw an old Robert Redford <u>film. It</u> was great.
Correct: Last night we saw an old Robert Redford <u>film, and it</u> was great.

GED SKILL FOCUS

Correct these sentence fragments and run-ons by adding words or proper punctuation. There is more than one way to fix each error.

1. Getting out of the habit of smoking.

   _____

2. After the Super Bowl game.

   _____

3. We live in Georgia we like the warm weather.

   _____

4. Some people have many pets others have none at all.

   _____

5. I worked hard at my job I did not get a raise.

   _____

Answers start on page 149.

Usage

Subject-Verb Agreement

The subject and the verb in a sentence must both be singular (referring to one) or plural (referring to more than one). That is called **subject-verb agreement.** To check that these two parts of a sentence agree, first decide whether the subject is singular or plural. Then make the verb match the subject.

Both singular:	The girl plays basketball at school.
Both plural:	The girls play basketball at school.
Compound subject:	The coach and gym teacher work with them to improve their game.
With interrupting phrase:	The students from their school come to games to cheer them on.

GED SKILL FOCUS

A. Underline the correct form of the verb in each sentence.

1. Basketball, a game watched by millions of spectators, (is, are) one of the most popular sports in the U.S.

2. Boys and girls (begin, begins) playing basketball with their friends in the schoolyard.

3. Almost every high school (has, have) a basketball court.

4. Basketball players (compete, competes) in the Olympics.

5. A basketball team (consist, consists) of five players.

6. The players, who want to keep the ball out of the other team's hands, (move, moves) the ball by passing or dribbling it.

7. A referee, two timers, two scorers, and an umpire (is, are) the officials of the game.

B. Correct the errors in subject-verb agreement in the paragraph below. Cross out incorrect verbs and write the correct verbs above them. There are three errors.

The game of basketball is not limited to the able-bodied. Handicapped people also plays on basketball courts around the country. There are special accommodations to make the sport appropriate. Partially blind players, for example, uses large balls with stripes or bright colors. For people with more severe visual impairment, rattles and bells is placed inside the balls.

Answers start on page 149.

Verb Tenses

Verbs change to show different times—past, present, or future. These times are called **verb tenses.**

Present:	Some people <u>move</u> very frequently.
Past:	Last year we <u>moved</u> from Toledo to Pittsburgh.
Future:	Next year we <u>will move</u> to Dallas.
Present Perfect:	We <u>have moved</u> four times in the past six years.
Past Perfect:	We <u>had moved</u> from L.A. when we came to Toledo.

Words and phrases within a sentence and in other sentences give clues about which tense to use.

GED SKILL FOCUS

A. Underline the correct verb tense to use in each sentence.

1. Last year, we took the plunge and (decided, had decided) to move to a new apartment.

2. The worst part about moving (is, was) that we had a lot of things to pack.

3. We (lived, had lived) in our apartment for many years, and we rarely threw things out.

4. The cost of a moving van (was, has been) very high.

5. We didn't have a lot of money, so we (ask, asked) our friends to help us.

6. My best friend said, "I (arrive, will arrive) at 9 A.M. on moving day."

7. We knew it would be a hot day, so we (bought, have bought) soft drinks for our helpers.

8. Our friends (help, helped) us load the minivan and carry our boxes up the stairs in the new place.

9. We (had lived, have lived) in our new apartment for six months now.

10. I don't think we (move, will move) again for a very long time!

B. Edit this paragraph for errors in verb tense. There are six errors.

When my family moves to the United States, I was only 12. I have left behind a lot of good friends in Colombia, so it was a very difficult transition for me. I don't speak English very well at that time. I found New York City very overwhelming. I have never seen so many tall buildings before. Now, when I look back, it's hard to believe that life is so difficult for me when I first came here. I have become a citizen next week!

Answers start on page 149.

Pronouns

A **personal pronoun** is a word that can be used in place of the name of a person, place, or thing. A personal pronoun can be a subject or an object, or it can show possession.

Subject Pronouns		Object Pronouns		Possessive Pronouns	
Singular	**Plural**	**Singular**	**Plural**	**Singular**	**Plural**
I	we	me	us	my, mine	our, ours
you	you	you	you	your, yours	your, yours
he, she, it	they	him, her, it	them	his, her, hers, its	their, theirs

Subject Pronouns
Singular: I am going to the beach today.
Plural: We are going as a family.

Object Pronouns
Singular: Jessie gave her a towel to bring.
Plural: The kids are bringing some toys with them.

Possessive Pronouns
Singular: That swimsuit is yours.
Plural: The boys have their trunks on.

GED SKILL FOCUS

Change the underlined words in the paragraphs below to pronouns.

A.   The Miltons are very fortunate, because the Miltons' apartment is near a beach. The Miltons live in Miami, within walking distance from the ocean. Katie Milton spends hours at the waterfront with Katie Milton's friends. Katie is an excellent swimmer and sometimes works as a lifeguard. Katie loves her part-time job, and she is very good at her part-time job. One day when a boy was having some trouble in the water, Katie saved the boy. The boy was very grateful. Another time, two children wandered away, and Katie helped find the children.

B.   Chicago's lakefront is one of Chicago's great assets. Whether people are rich or poor, people can go to the beach and get some relief from the heat. The bicycle path that runs along the lakefront is beautiful, and on Sundays the bicycle path is teeming with people enjoying the fresh air. Children can play with children's friends in the many parks that line the lakeshore. There's something for everyone!

Answers start on page 149.

Mechanics

Capitalization

RULE 1 Capitalize a **proper noun,** a word that names a specific person, place, group, or thing.

People:	Dolly Parton, Harry Potter
Places:	Canada, New England, Rocky Mountains, Elm Street
Groups:	the Democrats, the Rolling Stones
Things:	the Watermelon Festival

RULE 2 Capitalize a **proper adjective,** a descriptive word that comes from the name of a specific person or place.

Vietnamese people   the English language   American culture

RULE 3 Capitalize a title that comes directly before a person's name.

Ms. Serena Williams   Dr. Nolan Harris   Senator Untermeyer

Titles and family names (such as *mother, father, grandmother*) are capitalized when they are used to address a person directly.

"I'm sorry, Grandma, but I have to hang up now."

RULE 4 Capitalize the days of the week, the months of the year, and holidays.

Tuesday   April   Christmas   Memorial Day   New Year's Day

RULE 5 Don't capitalize a title or a family name that is preceded by *a, the,* or a possessive pronoun such as *my.*

Incorrect:	Bill has a <u>D</u>octor's appointment tomorrow.
Correct:	Bill has a <u>d</u>octor's appointment tomorrow.
Correct:	Bill has an appointment with <u>D</u>octor <u>K</u>lein.

RULE 6 Don't capitalize the names of seasons.

Incorrect:	Dr. Klein will move to a new office this <u>S</u>ummer.
Correct:	Dr. Klein will move to a new office this <u>s</u>ummer.

RULE 7 Don't capitalize a school subject unless it is the name of a specific course or a language.

Incorrect:	Medical students should have a good background in <u>B</u>iology.
Correct:	Medical students should have a good background in <u>b</u>iology.
Correct:	When Dr. Klein was in college, she took <u>B</u>iology 101.

A. Cross out the lowercase letters that should be capitalized and write the capital letters above them.

1. Many kids today watch cartoons like bugs bunny on saturday mornings.

2. An article in the *new york times* reported that several doctors, including dr. howard bookman, think young children should use their imaginations instead of watching television.

3. The american pioneers took many months to travel across the country in their covered wagons.

4. Today you can drive a car from new york to san francisco in less than a week.

5. School children have vacation in the months of november and december for thanksgiving and winter holidays.

6. Does anyone still take shop class or study latin in school?

7. The humane society takes in stray animals.

8. If the boston city council lets the boston symphony orchestra play in the park, should michael jackson be allowed to perform there, too?

9. I have appointments to see my doctor, my lawyer, and my dentist, dr. james street.

10. I hope to travel to france someday to see the eiffel tower.

11. My mother's sister, aunt kate, has a party every fourth of july.

12. On my block are a korean grocery and a thai restaurant.

13. Last year, we visited the grand canyon during our summer vacation.

B. Find and correct the errors in capitalization. Some words are not capitalized but should be. Others are capitalized but should not be. There are 12 errors.

I am planning to take a vacation in april. I will visit my Uncle in cleveland. He is a Doctor at lakeside general hospital. Then I'm going away again in the Summer on Memorial day weekend. This time my travels will take me to washington. I'll go to a lot of Museums, like the smithsonian institution, and enjoy what I hope will be beautiful weather.

Answers start on page 150.

Commas

Commas are like road signs. They show the reader when to pause to follow the meaning of a sentence.

RULE 1 Use a comma between items in a series—a list of three or more. The items in the series may be words or phrases.

> The recipe calls for <u>potatoes</u>, <u>onions</u>, and <u>cheese</u>.
> Steve likes <u>playing ball</u>, <u>jogging with his dog</u>, and <u>swimming</u>.

Items in a series should have a parallel structure. They should all be in the same form.

RULE 2 Use a comma in a compound sentence—two complete sentences joined by a conjunction (like *and, but,* or *so*).

> The young children played on the <u>beach, and</u> the older ones swam in the lake.

RULE 3 Use a comma to separate introductory elements—words or phrases at the beginning of a sentence—from the rest of the sentence.

> <u>Hey,</u> what are they doing to my car?
> <u>Because I didn't have an alarm,</u> thieves were able to steal my car.

RULE 4 Use a comma after a dependent clause that comes at the beginning of the sentence. A dependent clause contains a subject and a verb but is not a complete thought and cannot stand alone. It begins with a subordinating conjunction such as *if* or *since*.

> <u>After my car was stolen,</u> I began to take public transportation.
> **But:** I began to take public transportation after my car was stolen.

RULE 5 Use commas to separate a nonessential appositive from the rest of the sentence. Do not use commas for essential appositives.

Nonessential: Linda, <u>my friend,</u> gave me her subway pass.
Essential: My cousin recommended the <u>book *Protecting Your Car.*</u>

RULE 6 Don't use a comma unless a specific rule calls for it.

Incorrect: We sold our car, last year.
Correct: We sold our car last year.

A. Put commas where they belong in the following sentences.

1. The recipe is complicated so you need to follow it carefully.

2. Hey be careful! That pan just came out of the oven!

3. Anita forgot to wear an apron and her shirt got stained.

4. Since I live in a one-room apartment my kitchen isn't very big.

5. He read the recipe too quickly so he forgot which step to do first.

6. The kitchen was equipped with pots pans dishes and utensils.

7. He enjoys baking bread but he doesn't have much time for it.

8. When he got a new cookbook for his birthday he was thrilled.

9. Tallie Hines a first cousin on my mother's side taught me everything I know about cooking.

10. To be a good cook you need to love food have good instincts and be unafraid to experiment.

11. If you want to be a professional chef you can go to cooking school or learn on the job.

12. Jeff went to cooking school after he got his GED and now he works in a restaurant.

B. Insert commas where they belong in the paragraph below. Cross out commas that do not belong. There are eight comma errors.

Raspberries are delicious but they are highly perishable. They crush easily, and spoil rapidly. If possible buy your raspberries at a farm stand since they are likely, to be fresher there. Pass over any boxes of berries, that show signs of mold overripeness, or leakage. Store raspberries in the refrigerator. Don't wash them, until you are ready to use them. Raspberries are nutritious because they contain potassium, Vitamin C iron, and niacin.

Answers start on page 150.

Spelling: Possessives

Possessives are words that show ownership. Make a noun show possession by using an apostrophe (') and sometimes the letter *-s*.

RULE 1 Add *'s* to show the possessive for a singular noun and for a plural noun that does not end in *-s*.

Singular Possessive: Mary's kids are spending the day with her ex-husband, Wes.

Singular Possessive: Wes's apartment is across town.

Plural Possessive: The children's father lives alone.

RULE 2 Add only an apostrophe to show the possessive for a plural noun ending in *-s*.

Plural Possessive: The kids' homework is already finished.

RULE 3 Don't use an apostrophe with the possessive pronouns *his, hers, its, ours, yours, theirs,* and *whose*.

Incorrect: Who'se turn is it to drive them home?

Correct: Whose turn is it to drive them home?

RULE 4 Don't use an apostrophe for a plural noun that is not possessive.

Incorrect: Her relatives' think it was a fairly calm divorce.

Correct: Her relatives think it was a fairly calm divorce.

GED SKILL FOCUS

Underline the correct word in each pair.

1. (People's, Peoples') reactions to divorce can be quite varied.

2. In my (grandmother's/grandmothers') day, few people got divorced.

3. The only divorce she knew of was (hers/her's).

4. Her (parent's/parents) reacted with shock.

5. Her (boss's/boss') reaction was not a pleasant one, either.

6. My grandmother moved in with one of her single (friend's/friends).

7. She felt that her whole world lost (its/it's) balance for a while.

Answers start on page 151.

Spelling: Contractions

A **contraction** is a shortened way to write two words by combining them and omitting one or more letters. Like possessives, contractions use apostrophes.

RULE 1 Use an apostrophe to take the place of the missing letters in a contraction: *I + am = I'm.*

Incorrect: H'es always been a reliable worker.
Correct: He's always been a reliable worker.

Most contractions combine a personal pronoun and a verb:

you've = you have	we're = we are
she'd = she had	he'd = he would

Negative contractions combine a verb and the word *not:*

isn't = is not	wasn't = was not
aren't = are not	weren't = were not
don't = do not	didn't = did not
doesn't = does not	won't = will not
haven't = have not	hasn't = has not

RULE 2 Do not confuse contractions with possessives that sound the same.

Incorrect: Your a highly valued employee, too.
Correct Contraction: You're a highly valued employee, too.

Incorrect: Be sure to put you're time sheet in the box.
Correct Possessive: Be sure to put your time sheet in the box.

TIP

Words such as *piece* and *peace* or *your* and *you're* are homonyms—words with similar sounds but different spellings and meanings. Know the homonyms you have trouble with and practice spelling them correctly.

GED SKILL FOCUS

Correct the contraction errors in the following paragraph. There are seven errors.

Due to an error in payroll, employees wo'nt receive their checks on time this week. Several time sheets we're not received on time. Late time sheets create problems for payroll. Please do'nt submit your time sheets late! Its essential to keep accurate track of you're hours and turn in your time sheets in a timely fashion. If you have'nt given us a time sheet for this week, please do so at your earliest convenience. W'ed really appreciate it!

Answers start on page 151.

Answers and Explanations

UNIT 1: PLANNING

Lesson 1
GED Skill Focus (Page 17)

Topic 1: describes
Kind of information: discuss the qualities of something

Topic 2: state your point of view
Kind of information: tell what you think about an issue and why

Topic 3: explaining both the advantages and disadvantages
Kind of information: write about effects

Topic 4: explains why
Kind of information: write about causes or reasons

Topic 5: tell your point of view
Kind of information: tell what you think about an issue and why

Lesson 2
GED Skill Focus (Page 19)

Many answers are possible. Here are some sample answers.

Topic 1
violent shows can make children violent
causes people to be less physically active
educational shows can teach
provides world, national, and local news
entertains; provides relaxation

Topic 2
may place too much emphasis on sports
may ignore family or other important areas of life
encourages supportiveness and team loyalty
brings fun and entertainment to your life
may cause you to spend money that is needed for other things

Topic 3
employers expect employees to have enough education to handle job tasks
can't compete with employees who are educated if you are not
best jobs go to the best qualified
GED or diploma shows you have ability to learn
GED or diploma shows you can persevere

Topic 4
teens identify with their music
brings young people together
violent lyrics may harm young people
some lyrics promote drug use
loud music can damage hearing

Lesson 3
GED Skill Focus (Page 21)

There are many possible answers. Have your instructor or another student evaluate your idea maps.

Lesson 4
GED Skill Focus (Page 23)

A. Possible main idea statement: There are many different reasons people become homeless.

B. and C. Your answers will depend on what you wrote on pages 19 and 21. Ask your instructor or another student to compare your main idea statements with your lists and idea maps.

Unit 1 Cumulative Review (Page 24)

1. explain your point of view

2. tell what you think about the topic and why

3. list ideas or make an idea map

4. write a main idea statement

GED Mini-Test • Unit 1 (Page 25)

You should have used a list or an idea map to gather as many ideas as possible. Then you should have written a main idea statement based on your ideas. Share your work with your instructor or another student.

UNIT 2: ORGANIZING

Lesson 5
GED Skill Focus (Page 31)

Many answers are possible. Here are some ideas.
A. Pets keep people company; pets don't argue with their owners; pets don't eat much; pets don't require clothing, furniture, or personal items; dogs and cats snuggle up with their

owners without asking much in return; pets miss their owners and greet them when they return; pets are loyal

B. **Group 1: Not expensive**—pets don't eat much; pets don't require clothing, furniture, or personal items

   Group 2: Not fussy—dogs and cats snuggle up with their owners without asking much in return

   Group 3: Easy to be with—pets keep people company; pets don't argue with their owners; pets miss their owners and greet them when they return; pets are loyal

Lesson 6
GED Skill Focus (Page 33)

Many answers are possible. Here are some examples.

A. **Benefits:** anyone can do it, including physically-challenged people; good workout for the heart and lungs; relief from heat

   Little Equipment: goggles, swim fins, kick boards

   Ease and Convenience: indoor pools; lakes, ponds, rivers, and oceans

B. **Personal:** feeling of accomplishment; feel comfortable around educated people

   Job-related: feel more confident about applying for higher-paying jobs; can expect more promotions

   Educational: can compete with other graduates; can read and understand a broader range of reading materials

C. Many answers are possible. Have your instructor or another student evaluate your groups of ideas.

Lesson 7
GED Skill Focus (Page 37)

A. **Topic 1**
   Organization: Order of importance
   Possible order of ideas: 1 Little Equipment, 2 Ease and Convenience, 3 Benefits

   Topic 2
   Main idea statement (sample): Passing the GED would offer a person many advantages.
   Organization: Order of importance
   Possible order of ideas: 1 Educational Reasons, 2 Job-Related Reasons, 3 Personal Reasons

Topic 3
Main idea statement (sample): Society's emphasis on being thin has positive but also seriously negative effects.
Organization: Contrast
Possible order of ideas: 1 Good Effects on Health, 2 Bad Effects on Individuals, 3 Bad Effects on Society

B. Many answers are possible. Have your instructor or another student evaluate your groups.

Unit 2 Cumulative Review (Page 38)

1. You should group ideas that have something in common and then label the groups. Try to make three groups.

2. To think of more ideas, you can reread the topic, your main idea, and your groups of ideas. Ask yourself *who, what, when, where,* and *why* about the topic; think how the topic affects you or the people you know; and try to think of things that you have read or heard about the topic.

3. Sample answer: Because the essay contrasts life in a city with life in a small town, the best method of organization is contrast.

4. Your order will depend on your ideas and how you feel about them. Have your instructor or another student evaluate your groups.

GED Mini-Test • Unit 2 (Page 39)

You should have grouped the ideas that you gathered in Unit 1 and labeled the groups. Next, you should have tried to expand your groups. Finally, you should have numbered the groups to show the order in which you would write about them. Share your work with your instructor or another student.

UNIT 3: WRITING

Lessons 8 and 9
GED Skill Focus (Page 45)

1. a. good work habits
   b. A good worker is someone who understands how important it is not to be absent too often and who gets the job done.

c. people lose jobs because they don't show up for work or don't work hard enough; managers need workers they can count on to show up; employers don't tolerate workers who sit around visiting

2. **a.** the endangered bald eagle
   b. It is ironic that Americans are directly responsible for making the bald eagle, their national bird, an endangered species.
   c. people have developed land where eagles nest; they've polluted water, poisoning fish eaten by eagles; hunters and trappers killed eagles

GED Skill Focus (Page 46)

1. **b.** Many manufacturers try to increase sales by offering money-saving coupons or rebates.

2. **a.** An organization will reward people who report information about crimes that have been committed.

3. **a.** A résumé is a tool that can help you get a job interview.

GED Skill Focus (Page 47)

Sample answers:
1. More than ever before, adults need an education to succeed at work.

2. Smoking is costly to your health and your wallet.

3. Getting out of debt may be difficult, but there are ways to do it.

4. Before you take a drug from your medicine cabinet, you should determine whether it is usable.

Lesson 10
GED Skill Focus (Page 49)

Sample answer for Topic 1:
  Some people complain that professional athletes make too much money. However, these athletes deserve every penny they get. Athletes work extremely hard, make many sacrifices, and perform important services for the community.

There is more than one appropriate and effective way to write each introductory paragraph. Share your work with your instructor or another student.

Lesson 11
GED Skill Focus (Page 51)

There is more than one appropriate and effective way to write each set of body paragraphs. Share your work with your instructor or another student.

Lesson 12
GED Skill Focus (Page 53)

Sample answers:
A. 1. Details: Leaving the world behind and escaping into sleep is vitally important to your health.

   2. Details: Trust is an important characteristic that can only develop through honesty.

B. 3. Examples: Car horns, engines, and other traffic sounds beep, roar, and chug along; refrigerators, fans, and other appliance motors hum, whir, and stir the air; people talking and yelling make loud and shrieking noises; music from radios mixes with sounds from television sets.

   4. Examples: Hurried people try to get ahead of you in line; they bump into you on the streets, on the subways, and in buses; they play music too loud and interrupt your thoughts.

C. Share your work with your instructor or another student.

Lesson 13
GED Skill Focus (Page 55)

There is more than one appropriate and effective way to write each concluding paragraph. Share your work with your instructor or another student.

Unit 3 Cumulative Review (Page 56)

1. I would include an introduction, body, and conclusion.

2. The introductory paragraph includes a thesis statement that tells the topic of the essay and the main idea. It includes a preview of the essay and sometimes background information.

3. I would write one body paragraph for each group of ideas I've listed. I would try to have three body paragraphs in all.

Answers and Explanations

4. I would use the label of each group to write the topic sentence for that paragraph. I would use the ideas in each group to develop supporting details.

5. Like the introductory paragraph, the concluding paragraph states the topic and reviews the supporting details. However, the perspective is different. Instead of looking ahead to these ideas, it looks back at them.

GED Mini-Test • Unit 3 (Page 57)

You should have written a five-paragraph essay. Share your work with your instructor or another student.

UNIT 4: EVALUATING

Lesson 15
GED Skill Focus (Pages 63–75)

Here are likely scores and explanations.

Essay 1: A likely score is 3. The essay is well organized with a clear presentation of ideas. There is adequate development of ideas, and many details are provided, but the language is too formal. There are some problems with sentence structure. The extra length of the essay would <u>not</u> earn it extra points from GED evaluators.

Essay 2: A likely score is 2. The writer states a point of view and provides support for a main idea, but there is insufficient paragraph development for an essay because there are too few details. The sentence structure contains errors.

Essay 3: A likely score is 1. The essay lacks focus, and the main idea is not stated clearly. The essay has limited organization. It fails to provide enough details and examples for the point of view. The writer has difficulty with the conventions of English, and the errors distract significantly from the essay.

Essay 4: A likely score is 3. The essay has effective organization, but the paragraphs are not fully developed. The essay needs more support for the ideas in the second paragraph. Errors in the conventions of English are present; there are several run-on sentences.

Essay 5: A likely score is 4. The essay has effective organization with a clear thesis statement and topic sentences. It has strong examples that support the main ideas. The writer has good control of the conventions of English. The revisions and messiness of the essay would not detract from its score with GED evaluators.

Essay 6: A likely score is 4. The essay has effective organization with a clear thesis statement and topic sentences. Several examples are given to support the topic sentences of the paragraphs. There are random errors in the conventions of English, but they do not distract the reader significantly. They would not detract from its score with GED evaluators.

Unit 4 Cumulative Review (Page 76)

Compare your answers to the evaluation checklist. Note the criteria that you missed.

GED Mini-Test • Unit 4 (Page 77)

You should evaluate your essay using the GED Essay Scoring Guide. Share your work with your instructor or another student.

UNIT 5: REVISING

Lesson 16
GED Skill Focus (Page 83)

Delete sentences off topic: "I own a car and so does my brother." (paragraph 1) "My favorite is country music." (paragraph 3) "Bus riding is okay." (paragraph 5) "My brother and I rode the bus everywhere before we got our cars." (paragraph 5)

Add more details and examples: Add to the second paragraph (for example, "you save time because you can come and go as you need to" or "it is safer to be in a car than waiting for a bus at night"). Add to the third paragraph (for example, "you feel more independent," "you can ride around with your friends," "or you can go for rides in the country").

Lesson 17
GED Skill Focus (Page 86)

Run-on sentences: The last sentence in paragraph 2 could be corrected like this: "In addition, they usually offer short menus. You can make a quick, easy decision about what you want to order."

The second sentence in paragraph 4 could be corrected like this: "The husband and wife are tired when they come home and don't want to cook. Instead, they want to spend time with their kids."

Sentence fragment: The second sentence in paragraph 3 could be corrected like this: "Hamburgers cost just a couple of dollars."

Verb use: The verb in the first sentence of paragraph 4 should be plural: "more and more families *are* made up of working couples."

Punctuation: Delete the unnecessary comma in the second sentence in paragraph 2: "by companies and along highways."

Spelling: The following words are misspelled: *It's* (paragraph 1), *finally* (paragraph 4), *therefore* (paragraph 4), *popularity* (paragraph 5).

GED Skill Focus (Page 87)

Delete sentences off topic: "Financing a house is extremely expensive these days." (paragraph 2) "Every time I go to the bookstore I see all these books about travel." (paragraph 4)

Add more details and examples: Add to the third paragraph (for example, "many charities help the poor and hungry and are always in need of more money" or "schools and college funds can use extra money, too").

Sentence fragment: The second sentence in paragraph 3 could be corrected like this: "For example, I would like to donate money to cancer and AIDS research."

Run-on sentence: The fourth sentence in paragraph 4 could be corrected like this: "I would never cook another meal because I would eat out every day in a different restaurant."

Verb use: The verb *come* in the first sentence should be *comes*.

Punctuation: In sentence two of paragraph 2, *parent's* should be *parents'*. Add a comma after the introductory word in the last sentence in paragraph 4: "Finally, I would buy. . . ." The last sentence in paragraph 5 needs a period.

Spelling: These words are misspelled: *college* (paragraph 2), *different* (paragraph 4).

Capitalization: The word *state* in sentence 2 of paragraph 1 should not be capitalized.

Unit 5 Cumulative Review (Page 88)

Your answers may be worded differently, but they should be similar to:

1. I should first revise the ideas and then proofread for the use of conventions of English. As I revise, I will probably cross some sentences out and rewrite others. It's more efficient to proofread when the text is in a more final form.

2. I can make changes by writing between the lines or in the margin, using a caret to show where additions belong, and crossing out any unwanted words or phrases.

3. I can use checklists on pages 80 and 84 to help decide what to change. I should also memorize the checklists so that I can apply them when I take the GED Test.

4. I can look back at my plan and check to see whether I included all the ideas in my essay.

GED Mini-Test • Unit 5 (Page 89)

After you have revised your essay, share your work with your instructor or another student.

UNIT 6: VARYING PREWRITING TECHNIQUES

Lesson 18
GED Skill Focus (Page 92)

There is more than one correct response. Share your work with your instructor or another student.

GED Skill Focus (Page 93)

There is more than one correct response. Share your work with your instructor or another student.

GED Skill Focus (Page 95)

There is more than one correct response. Share your work with your instructor or another student.

Lesson 19
GED Skill Focus (Page 96)

There is more than one correct response. Share your idea map with your instructor or another student.

GED Skill Focus (Page 97)

There is more than one correct response. Share your outline with your instructor or another student.

UNIT 6

Unit 6 Cumulative Review (Page 98)

Your answers may be worded differently, but they should be similar to:

1. To brainstorm, I would set a time limit and quickly jot down all the ideas that came to mind about the topic.

2. After brainstorming, I should judge my ideas and cross off irrelevant ones. When I brainstorm, I'm much more likely to list irrelevant ideas. I should cross them off so that I don't use them in my essay.

3. The six questions are *Who? What? When? Where? Why?* and *How?*

4. First, I would write down ideas about how the topic affects me personally. Then I would write ideas on how the topic affects people I know, and finally, how it affects society at large.

5. I would draw a circle and write the main idea in it. Then I would write a supporting idea, circle it, and connect that circle to the first one. I would write and connect details and examples to the supporting ideas.

6. Each label of a main idea group is numbered with a Roman numeral. Capital letters are used for the supporting ideas, and the details and examples are numbered with Arabic numerals.

GED Mini-Test • Unit 6 (Page 99)

After you have organized your ideas, share your work with your instructor or another student.

UNIT 7: RAISING YOUR SCORE

Lesson 20
GED Skill Focus (Page 103)

Having more leisure time can have both good and bad effects on a person's life. On one hand, more leisure time can improve the quality of many people's lives. They would have more time to spend with their families, to learn new things, to explore their creativity, and to travel. As a result, family relationships would improve. Additionally, people would become skilled in sports and hobbies.

On the other hand, too much leisure time can have some bad effects. People with little

imagination or low self-esteem don't always do well with time on their hands. In fact, some people become depressed or bored. Also, some join gangs or get into trouble with the law.

Lesson 21
GED Skill Focus (Page 105)

A.
1. F
2. O
3. F
4. O
5. F
6. F
7. O

B. There is more than one correct way to respond. Here are some examples:

1. Fact: Movies have been a popular form of entertainment for decades.
Opinion: The price of a movie is a bargain.

2. Fact: Attendance at sporting events increases every year.
Opinion: There's no better way to spend your entertainment dollar than at a baseball game.

3. Fact: A hobby such as hot-air ballooning is more expensive than one such as hiking.
Opinion: Everyone should take up a hobby.

Lesson 22
GED Skill Focus (Page 107)

There is more than one correct way to respond. Here are some examples:

A.
1. traffic: jammed, creeping, crawling, snarling, stinky, fumes, smog, stop and start movements, irritation, honking, yelling, bumper to bumper

2. telephone: ringing, buzzing, instrument, tool, attention-grabbing, annoying, essential, nuisance, talking, listening, waiting, dialing, means of communication, long cord connecting one person to another

3. money: crinkly, grimy, drab, green, essential, a must, problem solver, comforting, way to get things you want

4. summertime: sunny, blue skies, parched ground, steamy, splashing water, shouting children, ice cream, watermelon, snow cones, swimming, ball playing, camping, horseback riding, hot and muggy, like an oven

B. 1. Listening to music is relaxing.

2. Raising a child is demanding.

3. Crime is a serious problem.

Unit 7 Cumulative Review (Page 108)

1. The purpose of transition words is to connect ideas.

2. Possible answers include *because, to begin with, even more important, next in importance, the most important, mainly, finally, first, second, third, last*

3. A fact can be proved to be true, but an opinion can't.

4. Facts for the essay could come from the TV or radio news, newspapers, books, magazines, or from other reliable sources.

5. Opinions for the essay could come from your own beliefs or feelings.

6. Precise words are specific, exact language that expresses ideas more clearly and creates a picture in the reader's mind.

7. You could picture in your mind what you want to discuss, ask yourself questions, visualize actions, or think of words you have heard or read.

GED Mini-Test • Unit 7 (Page 109)

After you have planned, organized, and written your first draft of your essay, share your work with your instructor or another student.

UNIT 8: POWER Writing Review and Essay Strategy

GED Skill Focus (Page 114)

After you have planned and organized your ideas, share your work with your instructor or another student.

GED Skill Focus (Page 115)

After you have written your essay, share your work with your instructor or another student.

GED Skill Focus (Page 116)

After you have evaluated and revised your essay, share your work with your instructor or another student.

GED Skill Focus (Page 117)

After you have read and scored your essay, share your work with your instructor or another student.

GED Mini-Test • Unit 8 (Page 121)

Share your work with your instructor or another student.

Simulated Test A (Pages 122–123)

Share your work with your instructor or another student.

Simulated Test B (Pages 124–125)

Share your work with your instructor or another student.

Additional Essay Topics (Pages 126–127)

Share your work with your instructor or another student.

WRITER'S HANDBOOK

Sentence Structure

GED Skill Focus (Page 131)

Sample answers:

A. 1. a. Many people ride bicycles because they are a cheap, energy-saving alternative to cars.
   b. Many people ride bicycles, for they are a cheap, energy-saving alternative to cars.

2. a. Because riding a bicycle is good exercise, some people take up bicycle riding to lose weight.
   b. Riding a bicycle is good exercise, so some people take up bicycle riding to lose weight.

3. a. In Holland, there are bicycle lanes on many streets, while in the United States, bicycle lanes are more rare.
   b. In Holland, there are bicycle lanes on many streets, but in the United States, bicycle lanes are more rare.

4. a. After children learn to ride a tricycle, they ride a bike with training wheels.

   b. Children learn to ride a tricycle first; after that, they ride a bike with training wheels.

B.   Few people take a cross-country trip by train these days, but in the past, it was a common mode of transportation. Although a trip from Chicago to Seattle takes two and a half days, it is well worth it. On the journey, you pass through several mountain ranges and many picturesque towns. You may not get much sleep because you have to sit up the whole time, unless you have a sleeper car. However, there are a lot of interesting people to meet, so you'll be distracted from your fatigue.

GED Skill Focus (Page 132)

Sample answers:

1. It is hard getting out of the habit of smoking. *Or* Getting out of the habit of smoking is what I am working toward.

2. We are going out to dinner after the Super Bowl game. *Or* After the Super Bowl game, I will clean up the family room.

3. We live in Georgia. We like the warm weather. *Or* We live in Georgia because we like the warm weather.

4. Some people have many pets. Others have no pets at all. *Or* Some people have many pets, while others have no pets at all.

5. I worked hard at my job, but I did not get a raise. *Or* Though I worked hard at my job, I did not get a raise.

Usage

GED Skill Focus (Page 133)

A. 1. is

   2. begin

   3. has

   4. compete

   5. consists

   6. move

   7. are

B.   The game of basketball is not limited to the able-bodied. Handicapped people also play on basketball courts around the country. There are special accommodations to make the sport appropriate. Partially blind players, for example, use large balls with stripes or bright colors. For people with more severe visual impairment, rattles and bells are placed inside the balls.

GED Skill Focus (Page 134)

A. 1. decided

   2. was

   3. had lived

   4. was

   5. asked

   6. will arrive

   7. bought

   8. helped

   9. have lived

   10. will move

B.   When my family moved to the United States, I was only 12. I had left behind a lot of good friends in Colombia, so it was a very difficult transition for me. I didn't speak English very well at that time. I found New York City very overwhelming. I had never seen so many tall buildings before. Now, when I look back, it's hard to believe that life was so difficult for me when I first came here. I will become a citizen next week!

GED Skill Focus (Page 135)

A.   The Miltons are very fortunate, because their apartment is near a beach. They live in Miami, within walking distance from the ocean. Katie Milton spends hours at the waterfront with her friends. She is an excellent swimmer and sometimes works as a lifeguard. Katie loves her part-time job, and she is very good at it. One day when a boy was having some trouble in the water, Katie saved him. He was very grateful. Another time, two children wandered away, and Katie helped find them.

B.   Chicago's lakefront is one of its great assets. Whether people are rich or poor, they can go to the beach and get some relief from the heat. The bicycle path that runs along the lakefront is beautiful, and on Sundays it is teeming with people enjoying the fresh air. Children can play with their friends in the many parks that line the lakeshore. There's something for everyone!

Mechanics

GED Skill Focus (Page 137)

A.
1. Many kids today watch cartoons like Bugs Bunny on Saturday mornings.

2. An article in the *New York Times* reported that several doctors, including Dr. Howard Bookman, think young children should use their imaginations instead of watching television.

3. The American pioneers took many months to travel across the country in their covered wagons.

4. Today you can drive a car from New York to San Francisco in less than a week.

5. School children have vacation in the months of November and December for Thanksgiving and winter holidays.

6. Does anyone still take shop class or study Latin in school?

7. The Humane Society takes in stray animals.

8. If the Boston City Council lets the Boston Symphony Orchestra play in the park, should Michael Jackson be allowed to perform there, too?

9. I have appointments to see my doctor, my lawyer, and my dentist, Dr. James Street.

10. I hope to travel to France someday to see the Eiffel Tower.

11. My mother's sister, Aunt Kate, has a party every Fourth of July.

12. On my block are a Korean grocery and a Thai restaurant.

13. Last year, we visited the Grand Canyon during our summer vacation.

B. I am planning to take a vacation in April. I will visit my uncle in Cleveland. He is a doctor at Lakeside General Hospital. Then I'm going away again in the summer on Memorial Day weekend. This time my travels will take me to Washington. I'll go to a lot of museums, like the Smithsonian Institution, and enjoy what I hope will be beautiful weather.

GED Skill Focus (Page 139)

A.
1. The recipe is complicated, so you need to follow it carefully.

2. Hey, be careful! That pan just came out of the oven!

3. Anita forgot to wear an apron, and her shirt got stained.

4. Since I live in a one-room apartment, my kitchen isn't very big.

5. He read the recipe too quickly, so he forgot which step to do first.

6. The kitchen was equipped with pots, pans, dishes, and utensils.

7. He enjoys baking bread, but he doesn't have much time for it.

8. When he got a new cookbook for his birthday, he was thrilled.

9. Tallie Hines, a first cousin on my mother's side, taught me everything I know about cooking.

10. To be a good cook, you need to love food, have good instincts, and be unafraid to experiment.

11. If you want to be a professional chef, you can go to cooking school or learn on the job.

12. Jeff went to cooking school after he got his GED, and now he works in a restaurant.

B. Raspberries are delicious, but they are highly perishable. They crush easily and spoil rapidly. If possible, buy your raspberries at a farm stand since they are likely to be fresher there. Pass over any boxes of berries that show signs of mold, overripeness, or leakage. Store raspberries in the refrigerator. Don't wash them until you are ready to use them. Raspberries are nutritious because they contain potassium, Vitamin C, iron, and niacin.

GED Skill Focus (Page 140)

1. People's

2. grandmother's

3. hers

4. parents

5. boss's

6. friends

7. its

GED Skill Focus (Page 141)

Due to an error in payroll, employees <u>won't</u> receive their checks on time this week. <u>Several</u> time sheets <u>were</u> not received on time. Late time sheets create <u>problems</u> for payroll. Please <u>don't</u> submit your time sheets late! <u>It's</u> essential to keep accurate track of <u>your</u> hours and turn in your time sheets in a <u>timely</u> fashion. If you <u>haven't</u> given us a time sheet for this week, <u>please</u> do so at your earliest convenience. <u>We'd</u> really appreciate it!

WRITER'S HANDBOOK

Glossary

background sentences sentences in the introductory paragraph of an essay that give general information about the topic

body paragraphs the middle paragraphs of an essay which back up the thesis statement in the introductory paragraph with supporting ideas

brainstorming gathering ideas by writing down all the thoughts that come into your head without judging them

clarity clear presentation of ideas in an essay

compare and contrast a method of organizing the ideas in an essay to show how two things are alike and different

complex sentence a sentence formed by joining an independent clause with a dependent, or subordinate, clause. The subordinate clause has a subject and verb but is not a complete thought.

compound sentence a sentence formed by combining two simple sentences, or independent clauses, with a connector or a semicolon

concluding paragraph the final paragraph of an essay which restates the thesis statement and sums up the supporting ideas

contraction a shortened way to write two words by combining them and omitting one or more letters. An apostrophe takes the place of the missing letter or letters.

contrast to discuss different sides of a topic

develop to explain with details and examples

evaluating evaluating your ideas and organization; evaluating your use of the conventions of English

fact a statement that can be proved true

fragment a group of words that do not express a complete thought; an incomplete sentence

gathering ideas getting ideas about a topic by thinking about it for five to ten minutes and writing down your ideas

grouping ideas seeing what ideas have in common and putting related ideas in groups

holistically a method of evaluating an essay by judging its overall effectiveness

idea circle a diagram of nested circles that shows how widening groups of people are affected by something

idea map a way of recording ideas that shows their relationship to the topic and to each other

independent clause a group of words that has a subject and verb and that expresses a complete thought. A simple sentence is an example of an independent clause.

introductory paragraph the first paragraph of an essay, which tells the topic and main idea, gives a preview of the essay, and may provide background information

labeling groups naming a group of ideas to show how they are related to a main idea

list to write down ideas in the order in which you think of them

main idea the most important point you are trying to make

mapping a method of writing ideas to show the relationships between them

opinion a statement of preference or belief

order of importance a method of essay writing that starts with the least important ideas and ends with the most important

organizing grouping and labeling your ideas, expanding your groups, and ordering your groups

outlining creating an ordered list of ideas that shows how the ideas are related to each other

personal pronoun a word that can be used in place of the name of a person, place, or thing

planning understanding the writing assignment, gathering your ideas, and choosing your main idea

possessives words that show ownership

precise words specific, exact language

preview sentences sentences in the introduction that tell your reader what to expect in the essay

proofreading the second step of revision in which you evaluate and revise your use of the conventions of English

proper adjective a descriptive word that comes from the name of a specific person or place

proper noun a word that names a specific person, place, group, or thing

revising revising your ideas and organization; revising your use of the conventions of English

run-on sentence a sentence that combines two complete thoughts without correct punctuation or a connector

simple sentence a sentence containing a subject and a verb and expressing one complete thought. It is an independent clause.

subject-verb agreement a match between the subject and verb in a sentence when both are singular or both are plural

supporting details additional ideas that give more information about the main idea

thesis statement a sentence that tells the topic of an essay

topic the subject of an essay

topic sentence the sentence that tells the main idea of the paragraph

transitions words that make a smooth connection between ideas

verb tenses the times (past, present, or future) shown by different verb forms

writing writing your introductory paragraph, body paragraphs, and concluding paragraph

writing assignment directions to write about a given topic

Index

Language Arts, Writing, Part II, The Essay

Name: _____ Class: _____ Date: _____

_____

_____

_____

_____

_____

_____

_____

_____

_____

_____

_____

_____

_____

_____

_____

_____

_____

_____

_____

Continue your essay on next page

USE A BALL POINT PEN TO WRITE YOUR ESSAY

_____

_____

_____

_____

_____

_____

_____

_____

_____

_____

_____

_____

_____

_____

_____

_____

_____

_____

_____

MAKE NO MARKS IN THIS AREA

○○○○○○○○○○○○○○○○○○○○○○○○○▢